# Vegetables Naturally:
## An organic-gardening guide

# Vegetables Naturally:
## An organic-gardening guide

## H. G. Witham Fogg

Crescent Books
A Division of Crown Publishers, Inc.

*Acknowledgements*
The author and Publishers are grateful for the co-operation
of the following companies for supplying information and
photographs for this book:
Ferry-Morse Seed Co. (USA)
Thompson and Morgan Ltd. (UK)
Suttons Seeds Ltd. (UK)
Dobie and Son Ltd. (UK)
Burpee Seeds (USA)
Daenhfeldts (Denmark)

# CONTENTS

# CHAPTER ONE

# *Introducing Vegetables*

Some of the vegetables we now use every day as part of our meals, were once either shunned as food or used for an entirely different purpose.

For many years after potatoes were introduced into Europe they were not used in the human diet, but fed to livestock. Even then some people were prejudiced against eating the flesh of the animals which had partaken of potatoes, saying that the vegetables caused leprosy and fevers and that humans could be infected by eating them. One of the first to popularise the potato was King Louis XVI of France, who not only ate them with his meals but had large parts of his gardens planted with them just for the flowers, which he was so attracted to, that he wore a spray every day while they were in bloom.

During the reign of Napoleon Bonaparte the potato was widely used in France to make . . . a love potion. Josephine is said to have drunk it and so did many single ladies at Court who were seeking a husband. They also ate large quantities of potatoes for the same reasons, but it is not recorded whether it helped secure them a husband or made them overweight!

The tomato has a similar history. It was brought to Europe as early as 1596 from South America, but it was not until the eighteenth century that it began to be commonly eaten. Because it belongs to the deadly nightshade family, many members of which have poisonous properties, it was thought that the tomato was also poisonous. So it was grown as an ornamental plant for its flowers, scent and brightly attractive coloured fruits. The brave person who first tasted them is unknown, but afterwards a belief arose that eating tomatoes made a person temporarily passionate and so the fruit was given the name 'love-apple'.

Rhubarb now classed as a fruit, was used medicinally by the Chinese, as long ago as 2700 B.C. but although often mentioned in old herbals it was not grown in kitchen gardens for culinary purposes until the early nineteenth century. However, many old gardening books list varieties of the Russian and Chinese rhubarb being grown for ornamental purposes, the tall spike of whitish-yellow flowers providing an attractive feature, with the large leaves and rosy-red or green stalks.

Carrots were also grown in the reign of Charles II not only as a root vegetable but for the delicately cut foliage which young ladies attached to their gowns for personal adornment.

Onions were said to be a cure for all sorts of physical disorders. An onion cut in half and rubbed on the forehead was claimed as a headache cure, also if the heart was taken out of a roasted onion and put into the ear, as 'hot as could be borne', it relieved earache. More likely it was the warmth which did the trick. To cure advancing baldness the juice of a raw onion should be rubbed into the skin or thin patch until the skin is red and feels hot, according to an Oxfordshire remedy. Onions were also hung in doorways to scare off witches. The onion, due to its aroma, could hardly be thought likely to arouse thoughts of love, but according to one old country belief, girls searching for a husband had to eat plenty of raw onions probably because they are blood cleansers, leading to a healthy skin thus improving appearance.

Surprisingly some of our other every day

vegetables are associated with romance. Nine peas in a pod was considered a very lucky find. If an unmarried girl found one she nailed it over the door of the house. The first man who came through the doorway after that, excluding her father and male relatives, would become her husband. A pod with nine peas in it was also thought a cure for warts. The nine peas were taken out of the pod one at a time, wrapped in a pea leaf and buried in earth. When the last pea withered the wart would disappear.

If two single people ate the same lettuce, love would blossom between them or so it was claimed. In Medieval times, lettuce juice was also used in love potions and charms. Girls who wanted a husband also ate large quantities of raw lettuce, supposedly to increase their powers of attraction. This may have been true in the sense that lots of salad would cleanse the blood of impurities and improve the complexion. The snag was that the male admirer must also be persuaded to eat quantities of lettuce, and if he did then the power of the charm would be completed and they would be happily married.

Cabbage on the other hand, had a very different use and was far from being the humble vegetable we know today. The Romans thought it so important that it was included in their mythology, being highly praised and revered. This is no wonder, because at their wild orgies large bowls of raw wet cabbage leaves were placed on the tables to eat between the rounds of drinking revelry, the Romans believing that the cabbage leaves absorbed the fumes given off by the wine and so they could return home without any trace of alcohol on their breath. It was also believed that the cabbage would prevent a hangover the following morning.

Many plants apart from those generally recognized as vegetables can be eaten. These have health giving qualities as well as providing interesting variety.

Those who use what nature provides, are often looked on with surprise but with the cost of foods in shops steadily rising, a return to the wonderful herbs of our fathers of old can do no harm and may well yield inestimable benefits to purse and health.

In Europe in mediaeval times soups made from marigold flowers were thought tasty. Weeds such as fat hen, dead nettle, ground elder and samphire were brewed up too, to use as a stock while fresh shoots of bladder campion and sea holly were considered a delicacy. Wild asparagus can still be found, in some parts of the country and is delicious.

Salads so often based on lettuce, can be made more interesting by using pelargonium, nasturtium, or hollyhock leaves, toadflax, sorrel and the petals of calendula and nasturtium flowers.

Boiled bracken roots and young nettle tops have sometimes been used to replace cabbage. Love-in-the-Mist and nasturtium seeds can be used in place of capers. Berries need to be used with knowledge and care but non-poisonous ones such as berberis, elder and snowberries add variety.

As a change from tea and coffee dried goose-grass can be brewed or the seeds roasted to make 'coffee'. Some prefer mixing crushed acorns, broom seeds and beech nuts to make a beverage.

# CHAPTER TWO

# The Living Soil and its Improvement

Few of us realise how much we rely on the soil for our well-being. We should therefore do everything we can to conserve the soil's resources and increase its productivity so that the resultant rewards may benefit those who follow us. As Sir Albert Howard, that great conservationist once wrote, 'a fertile soil means healthy crops, healthy livestock, and healthy human beings'.

The soil is not inert dead material but contains myriads of living organisms which must be present if crops are to flourish. There are of course, many types of soil, including loamy, sandy, chalky or limey, clay and peaty but undoubtedly the best for producing vegetables, fruit and flowers is one in which there is plenty of humus.

Plants growing in chalky soils often suffer from chlorosis or yellowing of the leaves resulting in poor growth. Sandy soil dries out quickly, while clay soil may settle down like cement.

Working-in bulky, humus-forming material or 'ripe' compost will improve all of these soils. On naturally peaty ground which contains plenty of organic matter, some extra drainage may be necessary. The black peats are nearly always waterlogged whereas brown peaty lands are easier to cultivate and give better returns.

The land has to be fed. This can be done in several ways; by using artificial fertilisers, applying good compost, using farmyard manure, or a mixture of all these methods. Experience has shown that the continual use of bag fertilisers, will in time, lead to an almost lifeless soil that needs to be constantly replenished with the same fertilisers if it is to produce even a token crop of indifferent quality.

For too long, instead of feeding the soil, we have been content to feed the plants, where necessary often depending on artificial fertilisers in the belief that crops will be heavier and better. Organic gardeners know from experience that a good dark soil, rich in organic humus matter, produces better crops of higher nutritional balance.

Many gardeners can claim from experience that the free use of compost has produced better, healthier plants and well flavoured vegetables and fruits. Plants raised by natural methods are more robust and less liable to attacks by pests and diseases. Healthy crops used for food result in healthy human beings, for our health depends largely upon what we eat.

On how the land is treated will depend whether or not our food will contain its adequate supply of those properties which cannot be expressed in chemical formulae, but whose presence is made known by the good effect they produce on our health.

It is therefore necessary in the interest of quality as well as quantity, for there to be present in the growing medium, the right amount of humus, having the proper physical and biological content so that plants can function properly.

Because of wrong treatment and the urge to gain more rapid results the soil so often becomes exhausted before nature can replace the loss. This is why organically minded gardeners go in for composting, using animal and garden wastes of all kinds, including weeds and fallen leaves as well as kitchen refuse, to make a compost heap.

When properly made, after a few months these heaps become humus, the natural end result of all animal and vegetable decomposition.

A well-made heap engenders heat, which transforms the material into such valuable stuff with little or no smell and no flies. It is crops raised and grown in this natural humus-rich soil that are going to have the flavour that makes eating a pleasure. This is largely due to the action of living organisms including worms, bacteria, fungi and enzymes.

It is the effect of the climate over the years and the living organisms or agents that have built up the soil as we know it today. Earthworms in particular have played a great part by passing vegetable matter and soil through their bodies and drawing dead leaves and other material into their holes. They also aerate the soil, the tunnels they make allowing water to have a free passage. The greater the worm population the better the soil, for they breed and grow most freely where there are ample quantities of organic matter.

Generally speaking, chemical fertilisers discourage and may destroy worms whereas the organic gardener will want as many as possible in the ground he cultivates. The fine soil thrown up in worm casts is excellent for seed sowing.

Although we are prone to regard most fungi as undesirable, there are some species that are definitely beneficial. Among these are the mycorrhiza, a name which literally means 'fungus root', a term indicating an association of the roots of a plant with a fungus. In some cases this might be undesirable leading to wilting or rotting, but it is known that in certain instances, this association gives protection to the roots helping the plants to resist disease while compost encourages this working relationship.

Comparatively recently it has been discovered that certain soil fungi work on potato root eelworms preventing their increase and in that way act, as pest controllers as well as increasing general soil fertility.

Soil bacteria can be beneficial in promoting plant growth and general fertility. They obtain their nutrients and energy from decomposing organic matter. They multiply very rapidly and help to break down the soil through other organisms known as enzymes of which there are different kinds.

One kind of bacteria exists only in association with certain plants, notably the so-called legumes, including beans and peas. They form colonies that live in nodules on the roots. There, they multiply and absorb air nitrogen, transforming it in such a way that the plants can use it, thus improving soil fertility.

There are other soil organisms but these need not occupy us in our present coverage. What is important, is that the garden should have adequate aeration, good drainage and plenty of bulky organic matter, in order to provide conditions in which nature's workers can remain and increase in the soil and in so doing make it more alive and productive.

### How to Build a Compost Heap

The days when gardeners could obtain all the farmyard and other natural manures they needed for maintaining soil fertility are long past. Fortunately a first class substitute is available to those willing to make a compost heap and so convert garden and kitchen waste material into really good compost.

If the soil is to remain fertile, we must replace the natural foods that crops take from it and also improve its physical condition by incorporating plenty of organic matter. Well-made compost is a very satisfactory substitute for farmyard and other animal manures, and provides natural food whilst improving soil condition.

Decayed organic matter or compost provides humus which performs natural soil functions. It maintains the soil texture and provides plant foods such as nitrogen, phosphates and potash. Humus darkens the soil and so increases its power to absorb the sun's rays, so that it warms up more quickly in spring. It also opens up the soil allowing moisture and air to penetrate more quickly—most important points in the case of heavy or clay soils. In addition it improves the moisture holding capacity of light soils while it holds surplus nutrients for the future use of plants.

Fortunately a very wide range of materials are suitable for adding to a compost heap, not only the normal garden refuse, but vegetable peelings and other kitchen waste, tea leaves, household slops and the contents of the carpet

11

*Compost Bin*

sweeper. Tree leaves, straw, hay and bracken, green or dry can all be used. Woody material including cabbage and other brassica stumps should be well chopped or sliced before being placed on the heap, otherwise they will be very very slow in becoming decomposed.

The site for the compost heap should not be exposed to the sun, wind or rain, and under trees should be avoided. Where low ground is the only position available, it is unnecessary to dig a hole, otherwise water will collect and hinder decomposition.

On ordinary levels, make a shallow excavation for the base of the heap, and in very dry areas where rainfall is always low, pits of 18 to 30 in. (45 to 75 cm.) may be taken out. Fork over the foundation and if brush wood, cabbage stalks, coarse hedge trimmings or bricks are first laid into position, they will provide valuable aeration and drainage. Over these, place a layer of peat and well-rotted manure or even ripe compost. The various materials are then placed upon the base in layers, and it is best to mix the material well, so that decay is quicker and even.

The shape and size of the heap affects the rate of decomposition and the ultimate quality of the compost. For preference, make the heap in the shape of a pyramid without the apex or a rectangle avoiding a flat shapeless mass. For the average garden, a heap with a 10 ft. (3 m.) base tapering to 6 ft. (1·80 m.) and 5 or 6 ft. (1·50 to 1·80 m.) high is about right.

The ideal in building up the heap is to spread a layer of manure or soil, or to sprinkle dried blood or fish material or some other organic manure on each layer of waste matter, while a valuable addition to each layer is a good sprinkling of soil and ground chalk. Once completed leave the heap for three weeks then turn the material placing the outside in the middle. Then cover the heap with a layer of soil which will increase fermentation. In the case of bins, place straw or wood on the top.

Depending on the materials used, a compost heap takes anything from three to six months to mature. Heat from a well made compost heap is sufficient to destroy many weed seeds. Generally speaking, perennial plants which are producing their seed pods should not be used.

Symphytum peregrinum, better known as Russian Comfrey or simply *'comfrey'* is an excellent compost crop, providing several cuts a year. It has a high potash, protein and fibre content.

It is also used as poultry and pig food, while it has medicinal and veterinary uses. *Credit for distributing knowledge on this plant is chiefly due to the Henry Doubleday Research Association of Bocking, Essex.*

This deep rooted crop should be grown on a separate permanent bed, in a sunny position. Deep rooting, it can become a nuisance if placed near ornamental subjects. Space the plants 60 to 90 cm. apart, the richer the soil the wider the spacing. On good land and mulched with dried poultry manure, established plants will yield ten or more pounds at each cut, especially if given a dusting of slaked lime while dormant. Cut the stems when 60 cm. high and before they flower.

Before placing Comfrey on the compost heap, say one layer to four or five of garden rubbish, allow it to wilt overnight unless the material on the heap is already very dry. Comfrey can also be placed at the bottom of trenches made for planting potatoes, covering it with a little soil before setting the tubers.

## Compost Activators

Left to itself any accumulation of the organic remains of dead plants or animals will gradually decompose into humus and plant foods. The quality of such material will naturally vary according to the actual organic remains used, while some of the nutrients contained will be lost through the atmosphere or washed out or leached by rains and other weather conditions.

In nature, the breaking down process is often slow, so that if the material can be converted more quickly the richer will be the resultant compost in humus and feeding matter. Fortunately, decomposition can be assisted by adding an activator or accelerator to the stacked material.

To work properly, the breaking down organisms need both moisture and aeration; nitrogen being another necessity. In theory, anything of an organic origin can be composted, but some discrimination should be used. Young material breaks down more quickly

and is richer in nitrogen than older matter. Coarser plants, cabbage stalks and similar material should be chopped up and shredded and are best placed at the bottom of the compost heap.

The best way to hasten decomposition is to add an activator or accelerator to the stacked and moistened material. The decomposition is of a biological nature, accomplished chiefly by bacteria and fungi attacking and feeding on the organic matter which is then greatly reduced in bulk so that it easily mixes with, and feeds the soil. The rate at which this process occurs, partly depends on the presence of the right amount of heat and of nitrogen.

Sometimes the breakdown is slow which is the reason compost activators are frequently used. These lead to a rapid increase in bacteria which break down organic matter quickly.

There are a number of suitable activators and although inorganic substances such as sulphate of ammonia, nitro-chalk and nitrogen-rich fertilisers are sometimes employed, organic activators are much better. They are more gradual and gentle in the way they work, the resultant compost being better to handle.

Animal manures can be placed in 2 in. (5 cm.) layers between layers of plant material, as the heap is being built up. Poultry manure can be used more thickly. A dusting of powdered lime will be helpful in this case, since it will encourage worms and other beneficial soil inhabitants.

The Quick Return Method (QR) was developed by Miss Maye Bruce. For this, a herbal solution is added to the heap in accordance with instructions. This leads to the production of good quality compost which is ready for use in from six to eight weeks in summer, or twelve weeks in winter. The success of this method depends on the use of a wooden bin. The base should always be of earth which if of heavy soil, should have drainage improved with a good sprinkling of charcoal applied to provide sweetness.

Long material should be chopped up. For this method, do not use animal flesh, bones, dry sticks or tough kitchen waste. Tread down the material. Thin layers of manure can be used, but are not essential and light dressings of ground lime should be applied at each foot of the heap but do not apply manure and lime in the same layer. Keep the top of the bin covered with a sack, which will keep in the dry heat as well as killing weed seeds and preventing the top layer being dried out by wind and sun.

No turning of the material is needed and the Quick Return solution is applied, as layer by layer is built up.

The Indore method of composting as originated by Sir Albert Howard, consists of making a heap 4 ft. (1·20 m.) by 4 ft. (1·20 m.) and $3\frac{1}{2}$ ft. (1·08 m.) high. This should be enclosed by a timber 'box' made by nailing boards to uprights, leaving gaps each side between the boards for ventilation purposes.

Mixed vegetable waste should be placed in the box with up to a quarter of the same volume of manure. Add to this a little soil. Where fresh manure, which can be pig, poultry, rabbit or mixed is not available, fish manure, dried blood or hoof and horn meal can be used. Once the box is full, make several vertical holes in the heap to ensure a supply of air, then cover the top with boards or corrugated iron to keep out rain.

When fermentation commences, the heap will begin to sink. Add more material for rotting down and keep doing this until the box will not take any more. Leave the packed box for six weeks then take out and stack the material, leaving it to ripen for a further six weeks turning the heap twice during this period.

Seaweed extracts including *Marinure* can be used as efficient activators since they encourage bacteria that are particularly active in attacking fibrous organic matter and produce microorganic activity in the compost heap. *Maxicrop* in liquid form and *Bio Compost* maker are also good.

*Fertosan* is a bacterial activator for use in solution with water, while *Garotta* and *Adco* are other dependable organic activators applied in dry form. All of these are supplied with full directions for use and none attract house-flies, vermin or other pests.

# CHAPTER THREE

# How Plants Grow

Perhaps it is because the roots of most plants are underground while the stems, leaves and flowers are easily seen, that we rarely give sufficient consideration to what happens in the ground, and this in turn is the reason why we do not always ensure that the soil is in good heart.

We know that roots are essential and so often, when growth is poor or a plant dies, we refer to poor root action or root rots. Roots have two main functions—the anchorage of the plants in the soil and the intake of water and mineral salts.

In many plants anchorage is provided by one or more deep penetrating tap or thick roots, which have little feeding function but which hold the plants in position. From these tap roots, a number of tough supporting roots develop. It is the fine branching roots and root hairs, usually located near the soil surface, that search for and usually secure, the nourishment and moisture needed for growth. A root hair is a single elongated cell which thrusts its way between the soil particles.

This is why it is so important to encourage the development of fibrous roots and why too, gardening by organic methods is correct since it is in the abundance of well broken down humus matter that plenty of the finer roots develop. Consolidated and waterlogged soils do not favour root development through lack of aeration and good drainage.

The method by which feeding matter enters the plant is known as osmosis. This is the taking in of food in solution through the root hairs. When there is a stronger solution within the root hairs, this attracts a weaker solution in the soil. If highly concentrated fertilisers are applied to the soil, the balance is disturbed and the weaker solution then within the root hairs is attracted from the plant resulting in sickness and possible death.

There is reason to believe that some roots excrete or exude substances into the soil. Certainly living roots respire and give out carbon dioxide, and this with moisture, often forms a weak acid.

When roots die, they return organic and some inorganic matter to the soil, and these can eventually be beneficial to the next crops occupying the same site.

## Leaf functions

It is easy to forget or ignore the fact that plants, like animals breathe, taking in oxygen from the air and giving out carbon dioxide. This process releases energy and is of course known as *respiration*. Green plants also take in carbon dioxide from the air and give out oxygen. This is known as *photosynthesis* and takes place only in light and in the presence of chlorophyll, the green colouring matter based on a complex magnesium compound. During the process, carbohydrates form in the leaves and these are converted into soluble sugars which are transferred in solution to other parts of the plant. These sugars and other substances, along with the minerals absorbed by the roots, are used for the development of the whole plant.

Water plays an important part in the life of plants particularly as a carrier of mineral salts. The leaves also eliminate water which has been forced up from the roots. This is known as transpiration, a continuous process which increases in dry weather but becomes reduced in a saturated atmosphere.

Plants grown under glass will, if allowed, transpire more rapidly than the roots can absorb water. This leads to flagging or wilting. Their good condition can usually be quickly restored by overhead sprayings so that a damp atmosphere is immediately provided and loss of water by transpiration is rapidly reduced.

If we remember that leaves breathe, feed or assimilate and transpire, we shall become more conscious that plants are living and need certain conditions if they are to grow and function properly.

Close microscopic examination of the leaves of most garden plants will show they have breathing pores or stomata distributed over their surfaces, particularly on the undersides. It is these pores which open and close according to humidity, temperature and other cultural conditions and which therefore are concerned with assimilation, respiration and transpiration. This is one important reason for keeping foliage clean so that the pores can remain active.

Liquid plant food applied to the surface soil around the roots as well as foliar feeds can make all the difference between indifferent and first class growth and development. Provided the roots and foliage function properly and ordinary cultural conditions are observed, there should be no difficulty in obtaining worthwhile crops.

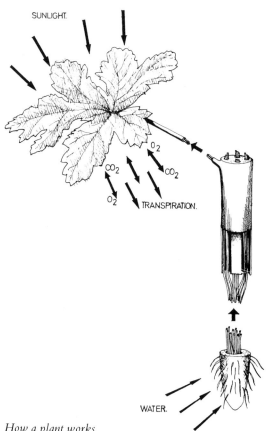

*How a plant works*

# CHAPTER FOUR

# Mulching and No Digging

The word 'mulch' simply means a layer of material placed over the soil, usually to cover the root area of plants. Mulching serves several purposes including the conservation of moisture and the prevention of drying out of the surface soil, especially where there may be only a few young fibrous roots. Some mulches are applied as a means of feeding plants, and with the application of mulches moisture from rain or water cans, infiltrates more readily without the repeated stirring necessary to keep the surface soil broken and receptive to water.

Mulches have other useful functions in that they help to keep down weeds and according to what is used, feeding matter from it is eventually washed down to a good depth. Earthworms flourish in the humus formed by organic mulching materials, making a further improvement to the soil.

Crops which are gross feeders will derive most benefit from a mulch of material which supplies plant food as well as preventing loss of moisture from the surface. When growing well, runner beans, late peas, cauliflowers, marrows and cucumbers, and tomatoes under glass, are specially responsive to mulching.

Do not apply mulches too early but wait until the soil begins to warm. The middle of May is early enough for cauliflowers, mid-July for runner beans and for peas, from June until late July, according to variety. Outdoors, tomatoes on light soil should be mulched by late June. Cucumbers under glass will benefit from several applications since this will prevent the white roots from surfacing.

Make sure the top soil is moist before applying any surface covering. Apart from materials which provide feeding matter and soil improvers, such as compost, leaf mould, peat moss and hop manure, there are many other materials which can be used. These include plastic sheeting which hinders weed growth; sawdust, although this leaches nitrogen which needs to be replaced and may also attract wood lice and ants; bark fibre and grass clippings, which sometimes become messy and harbour flies. Small stones too, can be used. Anyone who has moved stones in the dryest of weather, will have been surprised at the amount of moisture in the soil beneath.

The regular use of the hoe often produces a dust which acts as a mulch to the soil beneath; a practice once greatly relied on by our forefathers, so that while the addition of material with feeding value is much more beneficial and aids water retention, we should not too lightly disregard successful methods that have been relied on for so many years.

## No digging

For some years experiments have been made in growing vegetables and other crops by the no-digging method. This is not because certain gardeners are lazy and do not like the idea of the work involved in actually turning over the soil, but it is an effort to obtain the best results, and there are gardeners who have seriously tried 'no digging' and are unlikely to go back to moving the soil.

Instead of using a spade, fork or hoe in the autumn, the non-digger places a layer of compost all over the vacant ground in his garden. Advocates of this system, which in certain cases has much good to be said for it, argue that in nature plant wastes are not buried but become incorporated with the soil by the effects of the weather and the functions of worms and other soil inhabitants. Bulky material is reduced by natural decomposition without the help of man.

In addition, surface applications of compost provide the right conditions for the fungi which are present in fertile soil. Many weed seeds normally brought to the surface by ordinary digging could lie buried in unturned soil for many years, thus avoiding the necessity of constant weeding.

The success of the organic surface cultivation method really depends on the amount of compost available. Mulching places the raw materials where nature allows the natural workers to process it. Buried very deeply, organic material cannot be properly processed until it becomes near the surface again.

Among other advantages of organic surface cultivation, are that weeds are gradually eliminated and are not dug up again as is frequently the case with ordinary cultivation. Worms are not disturbed and therefore go on with their valuable work of providing soil ventilation, while soil bacteria are kept near enough to the surface to function properly.

Then there is the question of water supplies; the soil capillary working is retained, and moisture is drawn up from below. Plants grown by this method of cultivation show a vigour that is never seen where the gardener depends on continued supplies of artificial fertilisers, which not only cause the soil to become thin and lifeless, but never encourage the production of a bunch of fibrous roots, which plants need if they are to produce good crops.

There is reason to believe that surface mulching gives greater freedom from pests and diseases, while regular applications of composted material placed on the topsoil, results in better flavoured vegetables even though the size of the crop may sometimes be smaller.

It would be worthwhile trying a no digging experiment on a small plot to compare results with the more usual methods of cultivating the soil.

## Straw Walls

On very heavy soil, which is likely to pan or become hard and difficult for the fibrous roots to penetrate, results may be erratic and unsatisfactory. When this is so and the root system is insufficient, the foliage becomes sickly and there is little inclination for new growth. A quick way to overcome this drawback is by a method of incorporating straw into the ground. Wheat or oat straw is inserted in the soil in the form of vertical walls. This encourages aeration, helps to increase the beneficial soil bacteria, and allows moisture to reach the roots as required, promoting good growth.

The straw is applied as the site for the plants is being prepared, or it may be inserted by taking out trenches of sufficient depth to allow 5 to 8 cm. of straw placed vertically to protrude above soil level. A simpler way is to drive a spade into the soil and to move it backwards and forwards. The straw can then be driven into the soil with the spade.

Straw definitely helps in retaining moisture, an important matter particularly where the site is not on level ground. Straw treatment usually results in nitrogen shortage and it is advisable to work in dried blood, hoof and horn meal or any other nitrogen supplying fertiliser before cropping the soil again.

## Green Manuring for Fertility

While green manuring is most often thought of as a method of increasing soil fertility on smallholdings and larger acreages, it can also be done very successfully in the ordinary garden. Perhaps the most difficult problem is to be able to buy fairly small quantities of seeds although they can now be secured more readily than was once the case. I have used green crops for improving soil conditions in gardens and allotments in various parts of the country, and they have never failed to improve the ground and to make it possible for good results to be secured. There have been heavier crops of good flavoured vegetables and flowering plants, free from diseases and disorders, with blooms of good colour and texture.

Green manure plants are among the best natural soil conditioners. They improve soil tilth, chiefly by aeration and make it easier for other feeding agents in the soil to become readily available to plants. Green manure can

18

be said to grow humus which prevents plant foods from being washed out and in the case of legumes, they increase soil nitrogen without causing soft leafy growth, or encouraging edible crops to run to seed prematurely.

If in naturally clay soil the green manure crop is well worked in, it will break down quite fast and render the soil easier to work. Especially where there is not enough compost available for the whole garden area, a good biological fertility action can be built up with resistance to disease or pests by green manuring.

While it is possible to use certain annual weeds as a green manure crop and many of them are really fast growing succulent plants, some are liable to seed when quite small and a continual crop of self sown weeds can become a nuisance.

Green manuring is nature's method of gaining or increasing fertility and has many advantages. Whenever a piece of ground can be allowed to lie fallow for a period of six weeks or more of growing weather, the site can be dug or hoed deeply, and quick growing seeds to grow plants that make ample foliage can be used. These include, peas, beans, lupins, tares, all of which will add nitrogen to the soil. In addition, any flower and vegetable seed you have surplus to your needs will also help to make first class green manure if they are dug in when they are in leafy growth.

**Mustard** is often used and it is one of the best plants to grow when, for instance, one is using fresh land which has been stripped of top soil by nearby building operations, and one is left with an exposed lifeless subsoil. One should beware of using mustard where club root has been prevalent in a recently harvested crop. Since it belongs to the order cruciferae, it is liable to be attacked by club root fungus.

If dried sludge is dug in before mustard seed is sown, growth will be succulent and free. Although the humus that mustard supplies is not lasting, it is of special value when one is taking over a new or neglected site where the soil is dry and more or less lifeless. Since it is a quick growing crop, where the garden is not being used for some months, it will be possible to make two, perhaps more, sowings in the year.

**Sunflower seed** too can be highly recommended if the land is not being used for several months in early summer. This crop must be dug in before the stems become too tough, otherwise and they will take a long time to decay.

**The blue field lupin,** *Lupinus augustifolia*, has often been used as a green manure crop. The white flowering form is equally good. They are quick growing and ideal for sowing in spring or summer. Dig them in as soon as the flower spikes can be seen and while the stems are still fairly soft. It is helpful to first knock down the growths before chopping them up and putting them in the trench as digging proceeds. Any plants not dug in can be placed on the compost heap.

*Lupin*

The seed should be sown in the spring, spacing the rows 90 cm. apart, and finally thinning the plants so they stand about 75 cm. apart, in the rows. It is advisable to take out the growing points to encourage bushy plants to develop. The stems sometimes become very hard and when this is so, they should be broken down and the toughest pieces placed on the compost heap, rather than digging them in.

**Winter tares** are often sown in late summer, but they are equally suitable for sowing in spring when they can be dug in during the summer.

**Buckwheat,** *Fagopyrum esculentum* is another useful green manure crop. Since it is not a legume it is not attacked by club root disease. The seeds are large and are best sown in rows a foot apart. One ounce of seed will sow a row 34 m. long. Sown in spring, growth becomes very leafy, so much so that all except the coarser, more persistent weeds, such as ground elder, are smothered.

**Crimson Clover,** *Trifolium incarnatum*, is usually of annual duration and not to be confused with the clovers most of us like to keep from our grass lawns. If left it will grow 20 to 24 in. (50 to 60 cm.) high and as a bonus it will, if allowed to flower, be of use to bees which never fail to find and regularly attend the plants. For this reason, crimson clover is often grown near beehives. Sow the seed in April making sure the site is not lacking in lime.

The rate of sowing varies, but as a guide, mustard and vetches can be used at the rate of $\frac{1}{16}$ oz. lupins $\frac{1}{8}$ oz., peas and other coarse seeds 1 oz. all to the square yard.

Growth is usually quick and the normal practice once the flowers begin to pass over is to break down the stems and dig in the plants. If you can afford the space and the soil is in really poor condition, the site can be re-sown with the same crop again, which however, will mean that it will not be possible to use the land for an edible or ornamental crop until the

*Crimson Clover*

following spring. Another way of using crimson clover is to sow it in August or early September after a crop such as potatoes has been lifted.

Whatever green manure crop you decide upon, every endeavour should be made to take out deep rooted persistent weeds such as couch grass, ground elder, convolvulus, thistles, and docks before turning in the sown crop.

# CHAPTER FIVE

# *Vegetables and Their Culture*

**Alfalfa** is a salad plant which has long been recommended by nutritionists as having life giving properties inducing the body cells to remain active. It makes fresh green growth of excellent taste and contains a high percentage of protein as well as various vitamins. Professor P. R. Cheeke of Oregon State University, has discovered that when fed to animals, alfalfa contains cholesterol reducing agents with emerging evidence that these benefits extend to man as well.

Alfalfa seed can be sown in succession throughout the year and is ready for eating within four or five days, being particularly valuable as a winter salad. It grows best in a temperature of 19 to 22°C. and sprouting can be done in a jam jar or similar receptacle or on a muslin flannel in a saucer which should be rinsed once a day and then drained. Some herbs, such as chervil and sorrel, bring an added piquancy to almost any salad as does a suggestion of garlic.

**Artichokes.** *Cynara scolymus.* The Globe Artichoke has spectacular flowers and the foliage is ideal for floral arrangements. It is an evergreen and provides good ground cover.

Of upright habit the plants grow 1·20 to 1·80 m. high the well cut leaves, 60 to 90 cm. long, being greyish-green covered with white down on the undersides. The purple flowers produced at the end of summer are surrounded by an involucre consisting of fleshy scales which are the edible portion of the plant and which are considered by many to be a great delicacy. The flower heads should be cut with a short stem when young and tender, before the scales

are fully developed, otherwise they become coarse.

**Globe artichokes** are most suitable for growing in warmer districts where attention can be given to the covering of the crowns during severe weather. Strawy manure, bracken and weathered ashes are all useful for this purpose, although the covering is only necessary when

*Globe Artichoke*

Move the ground deeply during the early winter, working in plenty of manure or good compost. Roots or suckers can be planted throughout the spring. This will give a succession of heads from midsummer to early autumn especially if strong suckers are used.

Plant the roots firmly 75 cm. apart with 1·20 m. between the rows. It is possible to intercrop with lettuce, carrots or turnips the

21

first season but this should only be done when the land is clean.

In good soil, globe artichokes remain productive for five or six years. An annual winter dressing of decayed farmyard manure encourages good quality heads. Top dressings of an organic fertiliser in spring are helpful.

Always gather the heads when ready. If it is not possible to use them immediately, the stems can be placed in water where they will keep fresh for some days. After the largest central King Heads have been cut, side buds will develop.

Varieties include: Green globe and Purple Globe, the former being hardier and having fewer prickles. A particularly good well flavoured French variety, is Gros Vert de Laon.

**Jerusalem artichoke**. *Helianthus tuberosus*. This is the most popular of artichokes. The word Jerusalem is believed by some to be a corruption of an Italian word, girasole. The name artichoke was given to denote the similarity in the flavour of the tubers to the globe artichoke scales.

In drills or furrows about 15 cm. deep, place tubers about the size of a pullet's egg, 25 to 30 cm. apart. After covering them lightly work in fish manure or other organic fertiliser. A variety known as Fuseau is smoother skinned and therefore easier to peel.

**Chinese artichokes**. *Stachys affinis*. These produce ivory-white tubers which can be used throughout the winter, either cooked or in salads.

Growing about 45 cm. high they should be planted in spring covering the tubers with 15 cm. of soil. They do best in well drained loam. Wet soil causes the tubers to rot. The addition of peat or other humus forming matter leads to good growth and an easy to lift crop. Choose an open sunny situation spacing the tubers 45 cm. apart.

The tubers are ready for lifting from early autumn onwards, and should be stored in sandy soil or silver sand. Left exposed, they soon shrivel and become useless. It is darkness that keeps the skins white. Exposed to the light, they become yellow and less attractive.

*Jerusalem Artichoke*

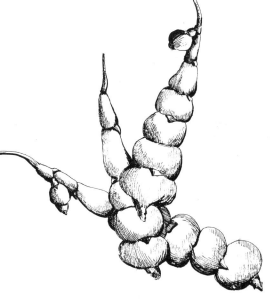

Although a hardy perennial plant, it is better to replant each year. Since they grow 2 to 2·25 m. high, the plants can be used as windbreaks, as a division or screen in the garden, or for protecting tender crops. This crop does best when grown in deeply dug, enriched medium to light soil. Fish manure well worked in is most beneficial. On heavy ground, the tubers are difficult to harvest and slugs may be attracted. Weathered ashes or silver sand used as a surface dressing, keeps pests away.

*Chinese Artichokes*

*Chinese Artichokes. The freely produced tubers can be cooked or used raw in salads.*

**Asparagus.** *Asparagus officinalis* var. *altilis*. This is usually regarded as a luxury crop which makes many gardeners shy of growing it. The wild species, *Asparagus officinale*, can sometimes be found but it is the cultivated forms of this species that are grown in gardens.

Cultivation is not difficult, but preparation of the site should be thorough, since it is usually possible to cut regularly from the same bed over a period of twenty years or more. For preference, choose a sunny situation sheltered from biting winds and move the soil deeply, taking out all perennial weeds.

The plants do best in rather light, sandy soil laced with organic matter although they can be grown quite successfully in heavy clay ground, providing there is good drainage. Sandy loams are best since they warm up quickly in spring and encourage the crowns into early growth. The prepared beds should be given a 13 mm. thick mulch of well rotted manure or rich compost, and the crowns planted in early spring, but so that they can

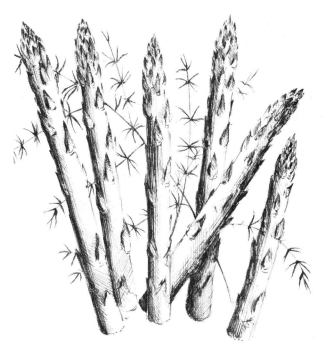

*Asparagus*

23

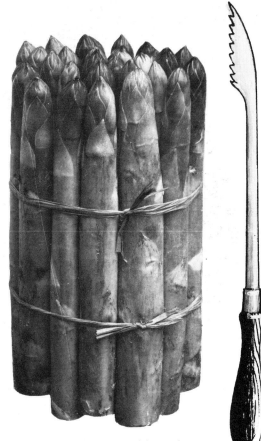

*Asparagus Crowns. As tied for market.*

crowns may be planted on the flat. When hoeing between the rows never go deeper than 5 cm. otherwise the shoots may be damaged.

Although not essential, a dressing of agricultural salt 2 oz. to the square yard applied in spring will be beneficial. It is best not to cut the first year after planting and then not to take more than two or three spears from each plant, leaving the thinner ones to mature into fern, which will help to ensure larger crops the following season. Cut the succulent shoots when they are about 10 cm. high, severing them well below soil level, using a special asparagus knife or something similar. On very sandy soil the shoots can be snapped off.

The foliage which is left to develop should be cut down to within 15 cm. of soil level when it becomes discoloured. Do not let any berries that form fall to the ground, otherwise useless seedlings may appear which subsequently become difficult to eradicate. This action will help to destroy the eggs of the only likely pest, the asparagus beetle, which may bore into the crowns that are left to develop, causing them to become brown. If the beetle is suspected spray the plants with Derris or Pyrethrum.

Asparagus can be forced in frames where a hot bed has been made. They can also be grown in boxes of not more than 30 cm. deep. Place a little good soil in the bottom, pack the roots closely together on this, and just cover them with ordinary soil. Moisten occasionally with tepid water, and stand in a temperature of 15 to 20°C. Forcing can begin as soon as roots can be obtained from the open ground.

Roots or crowns for forcing purposes must not be less than three years old and a supply for

become really established, no cutting should be done the first season after planting.

When planting the crowns take out trenches about 30 cm. deep making mounds of fine soil in the centre. On these, set the octopus-like roots 45 cm. apart. Then firmly work the soil between the roots finishing off with a depression to hold water should the summer be dry. The top of the crowns should be 12 to 15 cm. below soil level. On sandy, well drained soil, the

*Planting Asparagus roots*

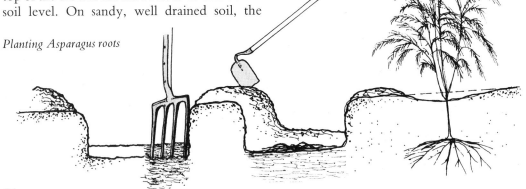

this purpose should be grown in flat beds. Where there are low forcing houses with side beds and hot water beneath, all that is necessary is to pack the crowns closely together on the bed. Cover them with the soil and mats till growth begins.

Success in growing good asparagus comes from planting top quality crowns, making up the bed correctly, and giving the plants ample room.

*Reliable varieties include:* Argenteuil, a variety of French origin; Connover's Colossal, the most popular sort with fine pointed buds; Kidner's Strain, highly recommended; Mary Washington and Martha Washington two American rust resistant varieties, but not so heavy cropping; White Cap, a high quality variety with pale green, almost white buds; and Giant French, a comparatively new variety of outstanding quality.

The soil should be prepared early and enriched with old manure and plenty of compost. Sedge peat worked into the top couple of inches of soil will be helpful. Sow seed in early spring using pots or boxes of sandy soil in a temperature of 15°C.

*Aubergine –*
*Egg Plant. Delicious when stuffed and cooked.*

**Aubergine.** *Solanum melongena* var. *esculentum.* Often known as Egg Plants, aubergines are worth growing on a limited scale. Ideal for cultivating in the warm greenhouse, they can be grown outdoors, in sheltered districts, once risk of frosts has passed. Frames and cloches also provide good growing conditions.

The soil should be prepared early and enriched with old manure and plenty of compost. Sedge peat worked into the top couple of inches of soil will be helpful. Sow seed in early spring using pots or boxes of sandy soil in a temperature of 15°C.

When big enough to handle, move the seedlings into 8 cm. pots or soil blocks, using fairly rich compost. By the end of April they should be ready to pot on to 13 cm. size pots. This prevents possible checks from starvation. Spray with water daily to prevent red spider damage.

Once warmer conditions arrive, the plants can be put under frames or cloches which should be kept closed for a few days so the plants settle down quickly. When they are 16 cm. high, take out the growing points.

When the resultant laterals have grown 10 cm.

they should be stopped. Allow up to six fruits to develop on each plant removing all others which attempt to form. Frequent overhead spraying will ensure that red spider does not gain a hold. Later crops can be sown directly into prepared sites under frames.

The fruits are ready to gather throughout the summer. They bruise easily and need careful handling. Usually offered as long purple or long white, Noire de Pekin is a dark violet variety, Blanche longue de la Chine being a good fleshy, white sort.

**Broad Beans.** *Vicia faba.* (Fava Bean). This is one of the oldest cultivated vegetables. Broad beans will grow on almost any soil excepting badly drained ground and land which dries out in early summer.

Deeply moved soil manured for a previous crop is ideal. Give a dusting of lime when the final surface preparations are being carried out.

Seed can be sown outdoors *from* early winter to spring or under cloches early in the year. Sown in spring the crop is likely to be poor and subject to black fly. Even for the November sowings, some kind of glass covering is useful.

*Broad bean*

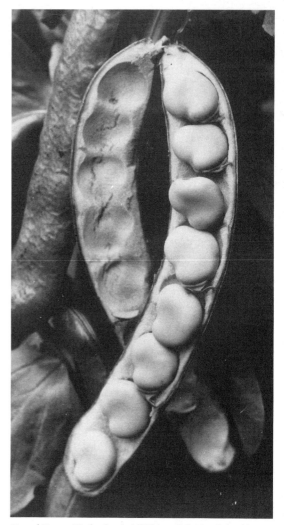

*Broad Bean, Eight Seeded White. Of splendid table quality.*

In all cases the plants need uncovering before growth reaches the top of the cloche glass. It is not worth making an autumn sowing in cold districts or where the soil is heavy and badly drained. If weather conditions prevent early outdoor sowings, seed can be started in boxes in a heated greenhouse or frame, for planting outdoors later.

For the earliest sowings use Long Pod varieties. These are hardier and heavier yielding than Windsors, which however, are of better flavour. Sow the seed 5 cm. deep in double rows, with 20 cm. between drills. Allow 75 cm. between each double row. Place the seeds zig-zag 15 cm. apart.

Dwarf varieties can have closer spacing. For the earliest sowings extra seeds should be sown at the end of the rows for filling gaps. As the seedlings push through the soil they should be slightly earthed up. This gives added protection as well as anchoring the plants. Earliest sown plants can be protected with bracken or straw during severe weather, removing the material when it becomes milder.

Keep down weeds by regular surface hoeings along the rows. Frequent inspection of the plants is advisable, so that blackfly can be dealt with by sprayings of liquid derris or a similar insecticide.

Once the first trusses of flowers are in full bloom, pinch out the tips. This will help pods to develop and discourage blackfly. Pest free

26

tips can be cooked and used like spinach.

Gather the pods while young, before the skins become tough. Early picking means good flavoured tender beans and a heavier longer crop. Sometimes when the main growth has finished cropping, a secondary basal growth develops and will yield quite well. The top growth of finished plants can be cut off and if the roots are dug in it will increase the nitrogen content in the soil.

*Broad Bean, Marathon. Heavy cropping and good flavoured.*

## VARIETIES

**Long Pods:** *Aquadulce Claudia*, very early. Seville Long Pod; Johnson's Wonderful; Exhibition Long Pod; Longfellow, heavy cropper; Red Epicure, with rich chestnut-crimson coloured beans or delicious flavour. Fenland Wonder, remarkably vigorous, heavy cropping. Colossal, one of the longest podded varieties. Outstanding for exhibition purposes. Imperial,

Green or White Longpod, up to nine beans in a pod, excellent flavour. Masterpiece, green longpod. A fine broad bean for early sowing and for freezing.

**Windsors:** The Sutton, 25 to 30 cm. high. Useful for the small garden. Dwarf White Gem, a green-seeded, small podded sort. Beck's Dwarf, an old but reliable variety. Green Windsor, excellent flavour.

**Dwarf French Beans.** *Phaseolus vulgaris.* Although usually referred to as French beans there is little evidence that they originated in France, in fact they appear to have come from South America reaching Britain by way of the Continent. They are sometimes known as kidney beans because of the shape of the seeds of most varieties.

The seeds can be eaten in the pod either green or dried. In the United States they are referred to as snap or shell beans depending on whether the complete pods are eaten as is more usual or the seeds.

*Bean, Goldcrop. Very productive, the well-shaped pods remaining in good condition for a long time.*

27

French beans grow on most reasonably warm and well drained soils. Early soil preparation is advisable, working in well rotted manure or compost. These beans make a good follow-on crop for brassicas, including Brussels Sprouts for which the ground has been well enriched. Bone meal or fish manure at 3 oz. to the square yard provides phosphates while lime should not be lacking.

In warm districts, sow the seed in spring waiting until danger of frost has passed. Make the drills 5 cm. deep, 10 cm. wide and 75 cm. apart, and sow double staggered rows spacing the seed 13 to 15 cm. apart. Allow for possible failures by sowing extra seeds at the end of each row. Avoid gluts by sowing small quantities at two or three weekly intervals until mid-summer. Very early pickings can be had by sowing under cloches or frames from spring onwards remaining covered until very early summer. Glass can also be used in autumn for covering a summer sowing.

The use of fine soil will give a more even germination without seedlings being deformed or broken from having to force their way through lumpy soil. Cover the seeds well, or birds will take them from the soil if they can find them. Keep down weeds and when hoeing draw the soil towards the plants.

Short bushy sticks placed at intervals along the rows will keep the plants upright and prevent the beans from trailing on the ground where they become soiled and a prey to slugs.

Pick the beans before they grow old and stringy. This not only ensures good, tender pods, but encourages the plants to keep on cropping. Under good cultivation, one may reckon that a double row will produce about four pounds of pods to the yard run of row.

An early crop can be produced by sowing in pots. A temperature of 15°C is needed and 20 to 25 cm. in pots are suitable. After crocking them well, half fill with J.I. Potting Compost No. 2 and sow about eight seeds to each pot.

*Bean, Stringless Blue Lake. Heavy cropping, quick to mature, ideal for canning.*

*Bean, Tenderbest. Smooth tender pods, almost stringless.*

*French bean*

*Seed drill taken out by draw hoe*

Wax or Golden Butter bean bears medium sized pods, as does Tender Green. Two very new promising varieties are Glamis and Glenlyon. In the USA some excellent varieties include Kentucky Wonder, Romano and Mc-Caslan.

**Haricot Beans.** These are dwarf French beans specially grown for their dried seed and not for pods. Sowing and culture is the same as for French beans, but the pods are left on the plants until they have ripened and turned yellow.

If all grow, reduce the number to the strongest six. Water carefully and once the plants have grown above the rims of the pot add more soil.

Support the plants with twiggy sticks and on bright days, give a thorough syringing. This will keep red spider away. When the pods have set feed the plants with liquid manure at ten day intervals.

Good varieties include The Prince which is almost stringless; Flair, an extra early variety with roundish oval pods up to 13 cm. long; Processor, excellent flavour; Pencil Pod Black

*Holding seedlings*

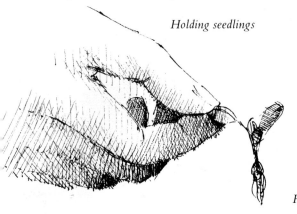

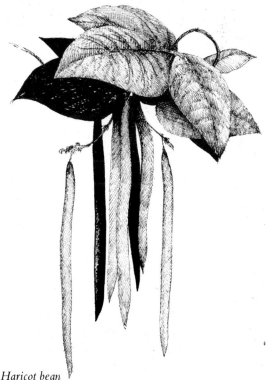

*Haricot bean*

29

They can be gathered individually as they reach this stage but it is easier to pull up the complete plants and hang them in bunches or in a sack in any airy place, to allow them to become really dry.

Once the pods are brittle the beans can be shelled or where large quantities are concerned, the pods can be carefully beaten with a stick which will knock out the seeds. Then spread them on paper or sacking in a cool greenhouse or other airy place to complete drying, when the seed should be really hard and free from mildew. The seeds must be quite dry before being stored in jars, tins or sacks, otherwise the beans will become mildewed and taste musty.

Varieties include Brown Dutch, a well known vigorous growing sort with yellowish-brown seeds. Comtesse de Chambord, strong growing variety, smallish white round seeds; Harvester, and Mexican Black.

**Soya Beans.** The plants grow about 45 cm. high, the foliage being a fresh olive-green. They flourish in light rich soil, full sun being essential, or they can be sown in pots in spring and be planted out when frosts have passed. Sow early, thinning the seedlings to 30 cm. apart.

The pods can be eaten green when they are about 8 cm. long and before the seeds are fully formed. The seeds are easily digestible and have considerable food value being rich in protein and high in vitamin content with an excellent flavour.

**Fiskeby V. Original,** is a recently introduced bean, related to the Soya. The seed is sown in warmth in early spring the crop being available in late summer.

**Runner Beans.** *Phaseolus multiflorus.* Although usually treated as annual, the runner bean is a perennial, forming tuberous roots which can be lifted in the autumn and stored for replanting the following spring. Excepting during times of seed shortages there is no advantage in doing this, for seeds sown in early spring give an abundant cropping the same year. Most varieties produce scarlet flowers which fact originally led to the common name of Scarlet Runner, although some varieties have white, or red and white flowers.

Runner beans can be used effectively as attractive climbing plants as well as producing

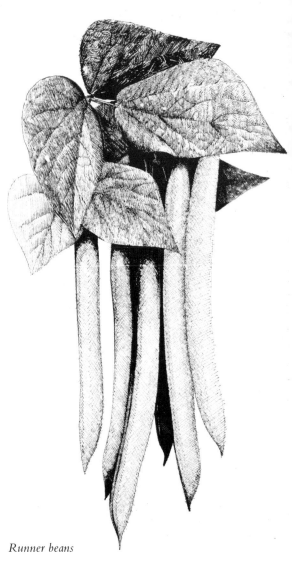

*Runner beans*

a heavy crop over a long period. They do best where they have a deep, cool root run. If possible, the ground should be double dug with decayed manure, compost, or other bulky material worked in. Apply a surface dressing of lime just before the seed is sown.

It is not advisable to sow outdoors until danger of frosts has passed. To make sure of an early crop, where a frame or a greenhouse is available, seed can be sown early in boxes 13 cm. deep, the seedlings being planted out after the frosts. Cloches can be used for standing over ground where the rows are to be made.

Good cultivation brings its reward, although for kitchen use, it is not the length of the beans that matters so much as straight brittle pods.

1) *Leek, Musselburgh.*
   *One of the finest with long, thick stems. Very hardy.*

*2) Showing a row of leek Marble Pillar, which produces
exceptionally long, solid stems.*

*3) Cabbage, King Cole.*
  *An early firm headed variety, taking up little room.*

4) *Cauliflower, All the Year Round.*
   *Large, white, well-protected heads. For frame or*
   *open ground.*

5) *Brussels Sprout, Early Half-Tall* (*Continuity*).
*Extra early, producing crops up to Christmas.*

*6) Brussels Sprout, Prince Askold.*
*A semi-dwarf, late variety with tight, solid sprouts.*

7) Above  *Beetroot, Formanova.*
   *Deep red with no white rings. Of excellent quality.*

7a) Below  *Radish, Scarlet Globe.*
   *Red skin, white crisp flesh. Of good flavour.*

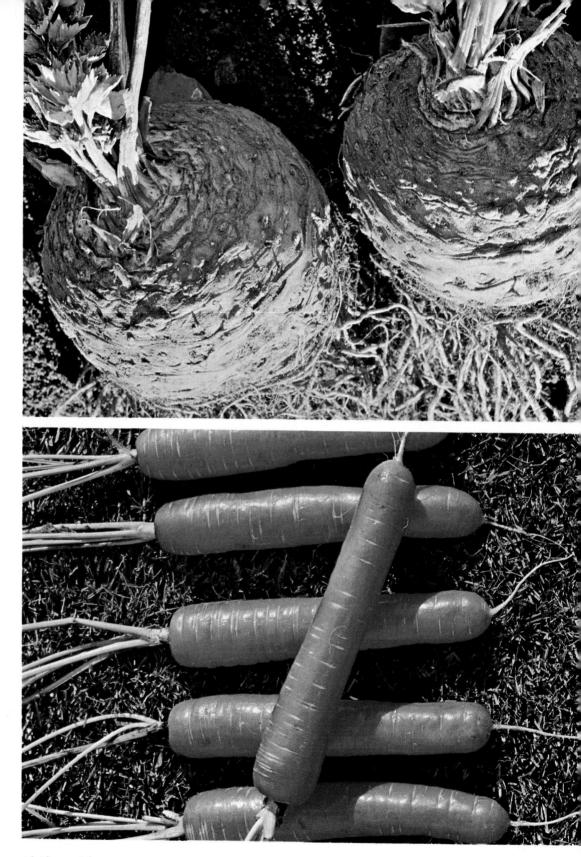

8a) Above *Celeriac.*
   *The turnip-rooted celery. Stores well. Can be used in salads or boiled.*

8b) Below *Carrot, Nantes Express.*
   *A most useful variety with little core. Can be forced.*

For exhibition purposes it is a different matter and there is keen competition to secure really long clean pods.

Deep rich soil is best and on light, sandy soils it is helpful to take out trenches up to 20 cm. deep and to place in them a really thick layer of compost, peat and other moisture retentive material with the addition of fish meal. Finish off the trench so there is a depression, for this will help to prevent the roots drying out during summer. On heavy land it is best not to make a trench but to dig the entire plot, otherwise the trench may become a sump for draining water.

Double staggered rows 23 to 30 cm apart in the trenches makes it easy for staking and where a quantity of beans are being sown, the double rows should be 1·50 to 1·80 m. apart. If possible, supports should be in position before the seed is sown.

Bean poles are very suitable and they can be placed upright or at an angle so the tops cross. Other poles placed through the tops of the crossed poles and fastened together, form a a strong structure. Alternatively, string or bushy hazel sticks can be used or a group of poles or strings can be placed in a circle and connected to one central pole to form a tent-like structure.

*Runner beans – Supporting of*

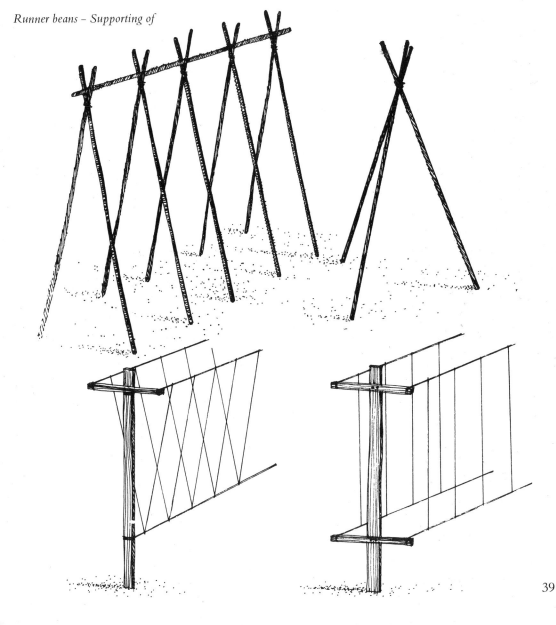

39

As they begin to climb, the seedlings need some directing so they do not grow into each other. It is possible to grow runner beans without any support and for this purpose the growing points are pinched out when the plants are 27 to 30 cm. high. The resultant shoots are also stopped and this leads to bushy growth, but heavier, more shapely and a cleaner crop is produced undamaged by slugs when supports are provided.

Frequent summer hoeings will keep down weeds and a mulch of leaf mould or strawy manure in early summer will act as a weed smotherer and prevent the surface soil from drying out. Harvest the pods regularly, otherwise the crop will be reduced. If the beans cannot be used fairly quickly, the stem ends can be placed in shallow water where they will remain fresh for several days if kept cool.

Frequent overhead sprayings of water during summer will keep the foliage in good condition and encourage a good set. The dropping of buds and flowers before the pods develop, is often due to a dry atmosphere and the absence of pollenating insects. Overhead sprayings help to distribute the pollen.

Many varieties are available, including: Achievement, Best of All, Crusader, Prizewinner, Scarlet Emperor, Streamline, White Achievement and Yard Stick, the latter being a particularly good variety for exhibitors.

**The Kentucky Wonder** bean is most popular in the United States where it is known as a 'pole bean'. It is a heavy cropper with the distinction of the pods remaining stringless, brittle and tender even when they become old.

**Hammond's Scarlet** and its white form are dwarf non-trailing 'runner' beans growing about 40 cm. Extra early and excellent for growing under cloches, they do not need staking and produce 20 to 25 cm. pods continuously over a period of ten weeks or more if gathered regularly.

**Climbing French Beans.** Very similar to the dwarf varieties but specially useful for greenhouse culture during winter and spring. For

*Double Digging (I) 10 in.–12 in.*   *Double Digging (II) Deep cultivation by double digging*

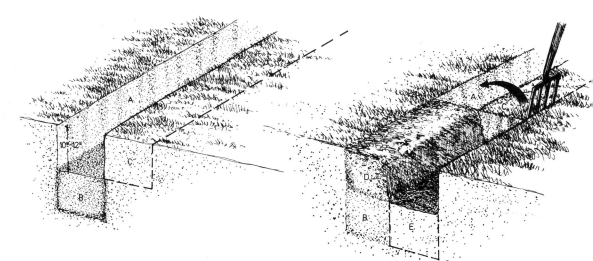

A. 1st Trench taken out

B. 2nd Spit of 1st Trench loosened to depth of fork

C. Top Spit of 2nd Trench

A. 1st Trench

B. 2nd spit of 1st Trench forked through

C. 2nd Trench top-soil moved forward to cover B

D. Soil from C

E. Bottom of 2nd Trench ready to be loosened up

*Runner Bean, New Twenty One. Strong healthy growing. Good flavoured pods.*

*Runner Bean, Sunset. Early maturing, heavy cropping, outstanding flavour.*

the earliest crops sow during the first few days of August.

A deep well drained soil containing a fair supply of organic matter is needed. Avoid the over use of nitrogen or the plants will become leafy at the expense of beans. Put one bean in each position where a plant is wanted, with a few extra seeds at the end of each row to fill possible gaps.

Climbing French beans can be grown in greenhouses which are wired overhead for tomatoes and the rows can be the same distance apart as the tomato plants. That is, a double row 45 cm. apart, then a space of 67 cm. and then another double row 45 cm. apart. The distance between the plants in the rows is 45 to 60 cm. For the supports, a stout peg to which is attached a T piece, is driven in at the end of the rows, to carry a wire 10 cm. from ground level exactly over the rows.

A single strand of tomato fillis is tied to this wire and to the top tomato wire, and the plants are trained up the fillis. A night temperature of

15°C. is required at all times, with a little higher during the day.

Good ventilation is necessary with frequent overhead sprayings of water to keep down red spider and encourage even growth. When the plants are climbing well and beginning to flower, less overhead spraying is needed.

The cultivation of a spring crop of climbing beans can be secured by sowing seed in the middle of February. If the light is very poor bean plants will not climb. Use pots into which three seeds are sown and ensure that the compost is nicely moist, so that watering is not needed until after germination has taken place. Cover the pots with paper and when the first pair of leaves have developed move the plants to their final positions. Outdoors they need a really warm sheltered site.

**Tender and true,** also known as the Guernsey or Jersey runner, is a splendid variety. It is early with clusters of long sickle-shaped fleshy pods of good flavour. Kentucky Wonder has clusters

41

of round fleshy pods, while Amateur's Pride is the climbing form of The Prince.

There are several interesting and good, but much less commonly grown varieties of climbing beans well worth growing. All can be sown in spring.

**The Blue Coco Bean** flourishes under the same conditions as the ordinary Scarlet Runner. It is a most handsome plant since the flowers and stems are rich purple, while the foliage is stained the same colour. The beans are produced in thick clusters and the purple shaded pods change to green when cooked. There is rarely any trouble from bud drop and the well flavoured beans can be stored for winter use.

**The Pea Bean** is not a cross between a pea and a bean but a definite form of climbing bean. The true variety has seed which is half white and half maroon and is of most delicious flavour. A light soil and unexposed positions should be selected.

**The Robin Bean** usually grows 2·10 to 2·40 m. high but will on occasion grow much taller. It is a variety for well drained soil and a sheltered position. This is a most ornamental variety, for the pods, fawn at first, turn to carmine or are splashed with carmine and have been likened to goldfish dangling on the canes. The seeds are also attractive, being prettily speckled, like a bird's egg.

**Lima Beans** are often listed as Butter beans and come under the class usually referred to as Dwarf French beans, all needing the same culture. There are some tall or climbing lima beans too.

**Beetroot** *Beta vulgaris* var. *cicla*. A biennial having a fairly long fleshy root, the bulbous shape which we now know, has been secured by constant selection and good culture. Excepting when grown for seed, the plants are treated as annuals and can be cleared from the ground within a few months from time of sowing.

Early soil preparation is desirable. A deep sandy loam which is moisture retentive is ideal. The ground should not lack lime and be well supplied with organic matter, either fresh or that given to a previous crop. Fish manure at the rate of 2 oz. to the yard run of row, is an excellent addition where dung is not available.

Make the earliest sowings in sheltered posi-

*Beetroot*

tions. For the maincrop select the round varieties, while the long rooted sorts and those for winter storage are for the later sowings.

For early pullings the rows should be about 38 cm. apart with 45 to 60 cm. for the maincrops. Thinning out should be done while the seedlings are small, subsequently making further thinnings, some of which can be used, if they are at least 4 cm. in diameter. The final spacing should be 4 to 8 cm. for the earlies and 13 to 15 cm. for the maincrops.

Light hoeing between rows is advisable in the early stages of growth but do not move the soil deeply. When the foliage becomes fairly large and the roots are swelling, soil movement should stop. This prevents damage to the roots. Left in the ground too long, beetroot may be damaged by wet and frost. Therefore, lift and

*Beet, Detroit Dark Red. A superb rich red globe-shaped all purpose variety.*

*Beet, Little Ball. Small smooth skinned, deep blood-red variety.*

*Beet, Formanova. Fine grained of excellent table quality.*

store the roots before severe weather arrives. Always handle beetroot with care to avoid bruising. The tops should be twisted off and not cut, otherwise they bleed and lose colour.

Store the roots in clamps of small size to prevent heating. Place them pointing inwards, in an orderly manner to form a compact heap. *Varieties.* Detroit Globe. Boltardy, Early Bunch. These are all good globe sorts. Formanova is longish-oval, whilst the old Long Blood Red is still good.

Recently introduced is Burpees Golden Variety. Of globe-shape, the skin is golden-orange the flesh yellow. The roots do not 'bleed' as do the red types. This variety has the advantage that the leaves can be used in salads or cooked as spinach.

Snowhite is another very new variety with crisp icy-white flesh and no bleeding. It can be used served cold in salads or boiled for use with fish. Excellent American varieties are Early Wonder and King Red.

*Beet, Detroit. Fine grained, sweet crisp flesh.*

**Borecole.** see Kale.

**Broccoli.** *Brassica oleracea botrytis.* These can very well be described as winter cauliflower and in fact they are now officially classified under the latter title. Most varieties of heading broccoli fold their leaves over the curds thus helping to protect them. Summer cauliflower leaves tend to grow upright.

Broccoli grows on many types of soil so long as it is fertile. An open, but not exposed position is needed, and one not likely to become a frost pocket. Freshly manured ground is not required. It is wise to plant broccoli after early potatoes, beans, peas or lettuce, and lime is required, otherwise disorders including whiptail may arise. A dusting of superphosphate and sulphate of potash worked into the seed bed provides the phosphates young broccoli need. Avoid fertilisers rich in nitrogen, for these encourage quick growth, easily damaged by frosts.

Bring the seed bed to a fine tilth, for this leads to even germination. Lumpy soil gives cover to flea-beetles. Sowing time is in spring onwards according to soil, weather and variety.

Make the drills 12 mm. deep and 20 to 30 cm. apart. Sow thinly and lightly firm the soil after covering the seed.

Keep the bed weed-free by frequent light hoeings or hand pullings. Ground reserved for broccoli should be well cultivated making the surface firm but not hard. Do not leave the plants in the seed bed too long or they will become thin and lanky, and never produce good heads.

Discard coarse, poorly shaped, badly coloured plants and any without growing points. Ideal seedlings have short sturdy stems, plenty of fibrous roots and four or five good coloured leaves.

During dry weather water the seed bed before seedlings are lifted. If it becomes necessary to plant during dry periods, water the seedlings in. The old practice was to 'puddle' the plants. It consists of mixing soil, cow dung and water in a bucket and putting the roots in it. This mixture clings to the roots and supplies moisture for some time. Puddled-in roots seem more susceptible to club root disorder.

Do not plant broccoli too closely. Smaller

*Broccoli, Rex. F.1 hybrid. Large uniform heads, slight purplish tinge.*

growing sorts should be placed 45 cm. apart with 60 cm. between rows, but most varieties need to be 60 cm. apart with 67 to 75 cm. from row to row. Close spacing prevents plants from developing fully and makes it easy for disease to gain a hold. Plant firmly and keep the hoe moving, particularly until the plants are established. Draw the soil towards the plant stems for this anchors the plants more firmly, giving protection and preventing moisture settling round the stems.

Cut the heads as they mature. Left too long they continue to grow and the good tight head of curds will open out and become 'ricey'. Early morning sun can damage the curds. To prevent this, heel over the plants in November so that the heads face the north. This is done by taking some soil away from the north side of the plants and pulling them over, then place the soil on the opposite side from where it was taken, making it nicely firm.

Should heads mature faster than needed, they can be kept back by bending a leaf or two over the centre of the plants, which also gives protection from frost. If the entire plant is pulled up and hung in a dry airy place the curds will remain in a good condition for seven to fourteen days.

*Varieties*. Autumn and winter use: Veitch's Self Protecting. Snow's Superb Winter White. St. Agnes. For spring use: Knight's Protecting. Leamington. Markanta. Armado May. For summer use: Royal Oak. Asmer Juno. Asmer Midsummer.

**Broccoli, sprouting.** *Brassica oleracea* var. *italica*. Wherever there is room, sprouting broccoli should be grown. It is hardy, of good flavour and makes a pleasant change, especially as it matures when other green vegetables are becoming scarce. The same soil preparation and cultural methods are required as for heading broccoli. Since the plants are fairly tall growing, they should not be placed where they are exposed to strong winds.

Seed need not be sown until spring, but early soil preparation is necessary. Farmyard manure or a good substitute should be worked in, a position manured for a previous crop being suitable. If necessary, a surface dusting of lime

45

should be applied before planting out. Over-rich land leads to soft, sappy growth, liable to winter damage. Sow thinly and transplant early, so that the seedlings do not become drawn. Allow 75 cm. between plants.

Sprouting broccoli is gathered when the flower heads are growing out of the leaf axils. If cut about two thirds of their length, more shoots will be produced from the base of the stems. Do not cut off the leaves since these afford some protection to the sprouts. although they can eventually be used.

As with other members of the brassica family, sprouting broccoli is much more palatable if steamed.

*Varieties.* Early Purple Sprouting, and Late Purple Sprouting provide a long succession of sprouts. White Sprouting is hardy and ready for cutting in spring. A well known USA variety is Spartan Early.

**Broccoli Green Sprouting.** Fairly well known as calabrese, this is an excellent vege-table for late summer and autumn use. It differs from the ordinary sprouting broccoli in that it first produces a good sized central head 15 cm. or more in diameter. When this is cut, the plant produces from each joint, shoots or sprouts which should be gathered when they have a 10 to 13 cm. stem. They become avail-able from early autumn onwards.

Under good growing conditions calabrese is very productive, more so than the purple and white forms, probably because it makes most of its growth during the better weather conditions.

There are now several strains including Atlantic, ready for cutting in the autumn from a spring sowing. Green Comet, is an F.1 hybrid giving a large central head, and Late Corona an F.1 hybrid which is later maturing.

*Broccoli Calabrese, Green Sprouting. The large central head is followed by a profusion of sprouts.*

**Broccoli Nine Star Perennial.** Although a sprouting broccoli, this plant provides heads rather like small cauliflowers. Since it is a perennial, the ground must be in really good condition at planting time.

Apart from farmyard and other bulky manures added when the soil is being prepared, a good dressing of fish manure or bone meal, say 3 or 4 oz. to the square yard, will encourage the production of the nine broccoli heads for several years in succession.

Transplant the seedlings to another bed so that they form plenty of roots and become sturdy specimens for planting 75 cm. apart each way in the autumn. The first heads will be ready for cutting in the following early spring. The seeds are not easy to secure at the present time but when available should be sown in spring.

*Brussels Sprouts*

**Brussels Sprouts.** *Brassica oleracea* var. *gemmifera*. This vegetable was known and cultivated in Belgium, particularly in areas around Brussels more than 750 years ago.

For best results provide an open, airy situation, with wide spacing, to ensure good sprout development. A long season of growth is required. For a really heavy crop highly fertile soil is necessary.

Deep, early cultivation should be carried out to allow the soil to become sweetened and well weathered. Firm ground is needed for good sized, tight sprouts cannot be obtained from hastily prepared, loose soil.

Sprouts do best where they follow a well manured and deeply cultivated crop. Where this is not possible farmyard manure and well rotted compost, say a bucketful to a square metre, should be worked into the ground in late autumn or winter. A dressing of an organic fertiliser such as fish manure, hoof and horn, or bone meal will be useful; hoof and horn in particular, supplying slow acting nitrogen, or one of the reliable compound fertilisers can be used.

Sowings can be made under cloches or cold frames early in the year. The seedlings should be pricked out 8 cm. apart in prepared beds under other cloches or frames, but must not be coddled. Subsequently move to prepared open ground sites.

*Brussels Sprouts, Prince Askold. F.1 hybrid. First class late variety.*

The main outdoor sowings should not be attempted before good weather in early spring. These can be followed by two or three sowings at fourteen day intervals. Open ground sowings can also be made in summer. Improved modern strains make autumn sowings unnecessary so long as early spring sowings are

47

*Brussels Sprouts, Early Half-Tall. Extra early of excellent quality.*

made in succession. Thin the seedlings out early to ensure sturdy growth followed by firm sprouts.

As soon as seedlings are 10 to 13 cm. high move them to their final position. Choose a showery period for the job or water the plants in. Space them 75 cm. apart for the dwarf sorts and 90 cm. for the tall, strong growing varieties. This spacing allows an early catch crop of lettuce, radish or spinach to be grown between the rows.

The plants can be helped by an occasional top dressing of organic fertiliser. Do not give this after midsummer, otherwise, leafy growth will develop and the sprouts will be loose and of poor quality.

Brussels sprouts like firm root conditions. Always remove loose, blown sprouts but do not cut off the top of the plants until all the sprouts have been picked. The head of the plant gives protection and helps in the growth of the sprouts.

Picking commences from early autumn on-wards and provided successional sowings of the right varieties have been made, sprouts will be available until well in spring.

*Reliable varieties include:* Early Half Tall, extra early; Peer Gynt, a good new variety with medium sized sprouts of fine flavour; King Arthur, a tall growing, mid-season hardy sort; Focus, medium sized sprouts of exceptionally good flavour; Roodnert Seven Hills, small tight sprouts of first rate quality, superseding Cambridge No. 5; Bastion, a very late variety with medium sized sprouts. There is also a variety with red coloured sprouts, although this is not widely grown. A reliable USA variety is Jade Cross Hybrid.

**Cabbage.** *Brassica oleracea.* The wild or sea cabbage is the ancestor of the present day forms of heading cabbage which is now recognised as Brassica oleracea var. capitata. Cabbages can still be found growing wild in many Mediter-ranean regions as well as on the southern coastal areas of the British Isles. Intensive

48

*Red Cabbage*

varieties, including savoys. Botanically the savoy is *Brassica oleracea* var. *bullata major* and it originated in Savoy in France.

Cabbages should be sown in prepared seed beds. Make the drills 18 mm. deep and 20 to 23 cm. apart. This makes it easy for weeding before the seedlings are ready for transplanting. Do not leave the plants too long in the seed bed or they may become thin and drawn with a poor root system. Lightly firm the soil after sowing. This assists germination and breaks down lumps which might provide cover for flea beetles.

Where possible spring maturing sorts should be grown on light soil. This warms up quickly and encourages rapid development. If cabbages follow a well manured crop such as peas or beans there will be sufficient bulk in the soil.

If humus is not present it will pay to work in decayed manure, compost or similar material. In the absence of any of these bulky types of manures, peat or leaf mould can be used, plus a good dressing of fish manure. If the soil is acid, a dusting of carbonate of lime should be

breeding programmes over many years, have given us the varieties we know so well.

Cabbages contain a fair amount of vitamin C. with smaller quantities of vitamins A. and B and also calcium and iron. They are usually divided or classified as—1 spring cabbage, 2 summer and autumn cabbages, 3 winter

*Cabbage, King Cole. F.1 hybrid. An early firm headed cabbage of exceptional uniformity.*

applied as a top dressing before planting out.

To provide cabbages throughout the year, seeds need to be sown at different times. For maturing from the late spring onwards, seed should be sown in summer when cabbages can follow early potatoes or peas. Make the rows 45 cm. apart, with 30 to 38 cm. between the plants. If in April the plants are growing slowly, an application of nitro-chalk 1 to $1\frac{1}{2}$ oz. to the square yard, will encourage growth. Plants which fail to heart may be used as 'spring greens.'

Summer and autumn maturing cabbages are sown early in the year under glass or outdoors when the soil is workable. Sow these little and often, to ensure that all the plants do not mature together.

Sow winter cabbages in spring and plant out the seedlings when the soil is moist. They need wider spacing than the earlier sorts. Make the rows up to 60 cm. apart, with 38 to 45 cm. between plants.

Late cabbages need extra nitrogen and more potash to enable them to withstand winter weather. Spring cabbages can be helped by applying a dusting of nitro-chalk along the rows.

Red cabbages are usually grown for pickling. Sow in spring for autumn use eventually spacing the plants 45 cm. apart. A summer sowing will provide much larger heads the following year. These plants are better after they have been touched by frost.

*Cabbages for spring sowings* for summer and autumn and early winter use include: Golden Acre, Earliest, May Star, Greyhound, Winnigstadt, Winter White and Vienna Baby Head. There are also a number of F.1 hybrids now available, including Autumn Pride, large, flat headed, maturing just before January King. Emerald Cross is also large, while Primata is early and of exceptional flavour.

Cabbages for summer sowings for cutting the following spring, include: Harbinger,

*Cabbage, Christmas Drumhead. Hardy, dwarf, compact and productive.*

Flower of Spring, Durham Early, First Early Market 218, and Hispi a valuable F.1 hybrid. January King is hardy for winter use and of savoy-like appearance. Among the red cabbage varieties are Niggerhead, Blood Red and the F.1 hybrid Ruby Ball.

Among the new varieties now on trial are Avon Crest, an early maturing spring cabbage producing pointed, medium-sized heads. It is also useful for cutting as 'greens'. Celtic is an F.1 hybrid winter cabbage producing uniform dense heads remaining in good condition throughout all but the severest of winters.

**Coleworts or Collards** are very hardy little cabbages which at one time, were largely used because they withstand the hardest of winter weather.

Sow seed throughout spring and summer. Later sowings will provide winter 'greens' since the plants may not have sufficient time to form a heart. For the quickest maturing plants sow where they are to remain to avoid transplanting. Seedlings should be thinned so that they stand 25 to 30 cm. apart.

If coleworts are planted between the larger growing winter and spring maturing cabbages, they can be cut before bigger specimens require more room. Varieties. Hardy Green, suitable for the later sowings or for winter greens; Rosette, for the main sowing and producing good heads.

**Calabrese,** see Broccoli.

**Sweet Peppers.** *Capsicum annum.* These are not cultivated as much as they deserve. This is because they are often thought to be 'hot'. If less pungent sorts are properly grown and cooked, they are a real delicacy.

Plants can be raised in exactly the same way as aubergines, spacing the seeds 2 cm. apart in pots or trays of good seed compost. Do this in early spring in a temperature of about 15°C. Prick off seedlings when big enough to handle moving them to small pots as they develop until they reach the 15 to 18 cm. size. Keep them in full light and spray with water frequently to keep off red spider.

If the plants are to be grown in a sunny sheltered position outdoors they can be pricked off into soil blocks of John Innes potting compost No. 1. Plants can also be grown under

*Pepper, Californian Wonder. A splendid variety for salads, curries and other dishes.*

cloches or frames, but must first be hardened off. It is best to plant in shallow trenches and to raise the glass when necessary keeping the plants covered throughout growth.

The plants grow 60 to 75 cm. tall, the white flowers being followed by fruit which colours according to variety. If plants fail to produce side shoots, pinch out the growing points. Once the fruit begins to swell, liquid fertiliser will prove beneficial.

*Capsicum*

51

Capsicums vary in length from 10 to 13 cm. In the case of the bull-nosed types, they are only 5 to 8 cm. long but much thicker and irregularly shaped. Chilli peppers are very hot and only used for flavouring and pickles.

**Green peppers** are the red and yellow sorts before they turn colour. Good varieties include: Canape with sweet, mild flesh; Burpee Hybrid and New Ace, a heavy cropper for glass culture. Some success is being achieved in breeding self stopping varieties which can be grown in the same way as lettuce.

*Capsicum, Canape F.1 hybrid. Early, suitable for frames or outdoors.*

**Carrot.** *Daucus carota. sativa.* A biennial plant producing flowers and seed in the second season, but grown chiefly for its edible roots. The carrot is probably unequalled by any other vegetable as a source of Vitamin A., while the roots contain quantities of Vitamin B and C.

There are white and yellow carrots but the orange and orange-red varieties are usually grown. Colour is important for it is directly related to the vitamin containing carotin, which is found exclusively in the outer layer of the root. Heavy foliage indicates a thick core, although the foliage should be strong enough to allow for easy pulling.

This crop likes a deep soil containing plenty of organic matter where the moisture content can be maintained at a good level. The use of fresh manure encourages the roots to fork and drought conditions adversely affect the size and texture of the roots.

Sowing time extends over a long period and in favourable seasons can start in early spring, using stump rooted varieties. To facilitate even, thin sowing, seed can be mixed with sand, which some gardeners make moist to encourage quick germination. Make the drills

TOP *Carrot, Parisian Rondo, Quick maturing ideal for forcing or outdoors.*

BOTTOM *Carrot, Danvers. Heavy yielding, of good colour, useful for freezing.*

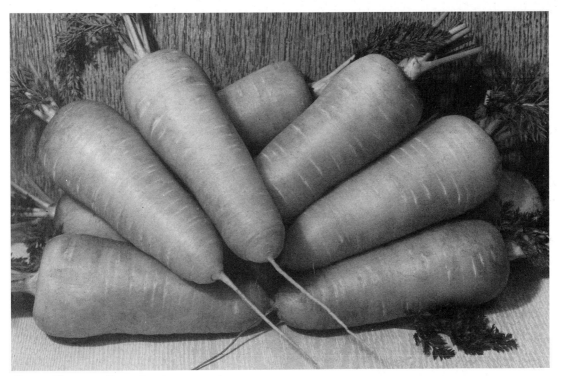

*Carrot, Chantenay Favourite. A most popular maincrop variety, excellent for exhibition.*

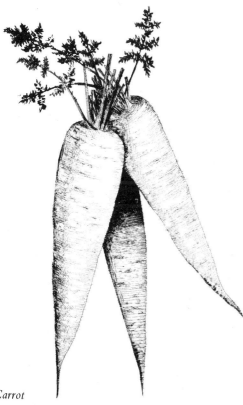

*Carrot*

2½ to 3 cm. deep and 30 to 38 cm. apart, lightly firming the surface after sowing.

Carrot fly can be a menace and is best controlled by preventative means. The pest is attracted by the smell of the foliage, so the crop should be disturbed as little as possible. This is why thinning is inadvisable since any open spaces in the soil allows the fly to lay eggs. Powdered naphthalene dusted along each side of the rows as a deterrent.

*Reliable varieties include:* Amsterdam Forcing; Early Nantes; Chantenay Red Cored; James Scarlet Intermediate; Scarla; Berlicum Cylinder, Goldpak, and St. Valery, a long variety. Parisian Rondo is a new round, quick maturing type for forcing or outdoor culture.

**Cardoon.** *Cynara cardunculus.* This near relative of the globe artichoke has handsome silvery fern-like foliage. It is grown for its blanched stalks which are not unlike the chards produced by globe artichokes. These are used in the same way as celery, in fact, both subjects require similar culture.

Cardoons like a rich, moist soil and succeed in trenches about 30 cm. deep and 20 cm. wide

53

where there is manure or decayed compost at the bottom.

Plants can be raised from seed sown in spring. They can be started over a gentle hotbed or in pots, but outdoors, wait until the second week in May before sowing.

Keep the roots moist throughout summer and applications of liquid manure will encourage good tender growth. The plants will be ready for blanching from early autumn onwards. One method is to tie all the leaves together and then earth up as for celery, or corrugated tubes can be placed over the plants. Alternatively, bracken or straw can be used.

The blanching process takes six to eight weeks and the stems should be dry before the operation begins.

*Varieties.* There are two main sorts. The French Cardoon, often listed as Tours, has long stems but their prickles make it difficult to work among the plants. The Spanish Cardoon is spineless but the flavour is not so good, the plants being apt to run to seed.

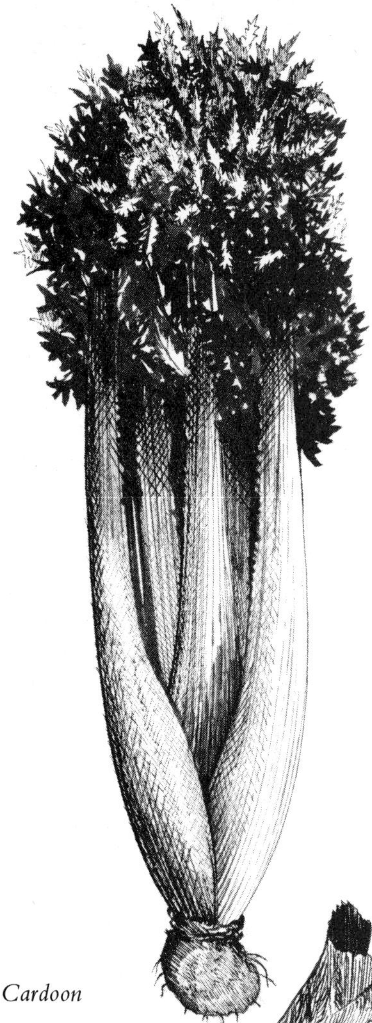

*Cardoon*

*Cauliflower*

54

**Cauliflowers.** *Brassica oleracea botrytis.* These are now known as Summer Cauliflowers and the plants for so long identified as broccoli are now to be referred to as Winter Cauliflowers.

It has long been believed that cauliflowers came from Italy, although a writer in the mid-sixteenth century says: "The seeds of cauliflowers come from Cyprus". The plant was described as the 'flourie colewort of which the small stems grow together in the centre, thick set and fast through together'.

This crop will not succeed in soils which dry out or lack fertility. The ground should be enriched with rotted manure or compost and although it should be well drained, a regular supply of moisture is needed. Bulky manures which increase the humus content greatly help to keep the moisture reserve.

Cauliflowers should not be grown in the same position more than once in three or four years. Prepare the site early leaving the surface rough and dusted with lime, unless the ground is known to be chalky.

The earliest sowings can be made in early autumn using a cold frame, cloches or the cool greenhouse. Make a seed bed, close the frames until growth is seen, after which ventilation should be freely given except during severe weather. This ensures good growth without softness.

*Cauliflower, Early September. A first class autumn variety of good flavour.*

*Thinning*

If the seedlings are thinned to 25 mm. apart they will grow into sturdy specimens for planting out in spring. Small quantities of seed can be sown in peat or soil blocks, making it easy to transplant without root disturbance.

Main sowings are made in warmth, the seedlings being moved later to frames or soil blocks. Seed can also be sown under cold frames. Sow outdoors when soil is workable with subsequent sowings at fortnightly intervals.

Sow thinly in drills 16 cm. apart; subsequently, thin the seedlings to 10 cm. apart before placing them in their final positions later. This moving breaks the tap root and results in the formation of many more fibrous roots.

The earliest cauliflowers are rather a fussy crop, needing care. At planting time look out for blind specimens or those without growing points. There are several causes of blindness, including a check in growth, sowing too early, exposure to frosts or severe drought. Blindness and buttoning sometimes occur after planting in the open and are usually caused by checks following cold winds or frosts.

With pot grown plants make sure that the roots are thoroughly moistened at planting time, for if the soil is dry the roots may fail to break out of the pot-shaped ball. Make the holes with a trowel rather than a dibber. The latter may leave air holes at the base which soon fill with water.

Do not plant when the ground is wet, and sticky. Make sure that the main root is actually pointing downwards and is not bent up in any way. Space the earliest varieties 60 cm. apart each way and allow 68 to 75 cm. between main crop and late sorts.

*Cauliflower, Polaris. Early maturing, large pure white curds.*

In dry weather leave a little depression so that the plants have the benefit of any watering or rain. Keep down weeds by regular hoeing and during drought, water may be necessary, for cauliflowers must never lack moisture or the curds will suffer.

When the plants are in full growth give liquid manure at fortnightly intervals, or a couple of dustings of weathered soot during the growing season will be of help. Dried blood is also valuable if applied at the rate of 2 oz. to the square yard and watered in.

Cut the curds while they are white. A leaf or two broken over the heads will keep them clean and white for some days, even during hot weather. If heads mature before they can be used, pull them up and hang in a dry, cool, shady place where they will remain in good condition for some time. Cauliflowers remain firm for a longer time if cut while they have dew on them.

*Varieties include:* Early summer maturing: All the Year Round, Dominant, Focus, Early London, Early Snowball, Le Cerf, Pioneer, Remme, Snow King and Snowflake.

Late summer and autumn maturing: Majestic, Novo and Walcheren. There are a number of good Australian varieties which are becoming very popular. These include: South Pacific, Canberra, Barrier Reed Wombat and the Flora Blanca varieties.

**Celery.** *Apium graveolens.* Garden celery is derived from the wild plant sometimes known as 'smallage' which grows in moist places in many parts of the world. It was grown in France and Italy in the seventeenth century but it did not become well known in Britain until the year 1800. A biennial plant, it is eaten raw or cooked, while considerable quantities are now canned.

For the earliest sticks, sow seed early in the year, making the main sowings three weeks

56

later. Sow thinly in boxes or pots of seed compost. Give a light covering of soil, then press the surface and apply a sprinkling of water. Cover with glass and paper and keep in a temperature of 15°C until growth is seen. Then remove the coverings and when the seedlings can be handled easily, move them into other boxes. After ten days, transfer them to a frame or cloches for hardening off.

Moisture loving, celery does best in peaty or similar soils where there is a high water-table.

An acid soil suits this plant rather than alkaline ground.

Celery is often grown on the 'flat' blanching being done by covering with 'collars' or even drainpipes. For finest results trenches are best. Make them 38 cm. wide for single rows and 45 cm. or more where double rows are being grown. Dig them 45 to 60 cm' deep and throw the soil equally on both sides of the trench, where it can, if required, be used to grow a catch crop such as lettuce or radishes. When growing a double row, place the plants side by side and not zig-zag as is usually done with a double row. This makes it easier for blanching. If more than one double row is grown, allow at least 90 cm. between them, or 1·20 m. if the soil is rich. Better plants are secured from single rows. Should side shoots develop pull them out.

As far as possible, lift the plants from the seed box with some soil on the roots. This will lessen the check. Unless it is showery, give the soil a good watering after planting firmly, and during dry weather, frequent sprayings will prove beneficial. Once established, the plants revel in plenty of moisture, while good growth can be encouraged by applying a well balanced fertiliser. Keep side shoots and decayed leaves removed. Weathered soot helps to keep off celery fly.

Blanching is done by earthing up, a process which must be carried out gradually. It is usually possible to add more than 15 cm. of soil at each operation, and it will have to be repeated at least three times, at fourteen day

*Celery*

*Earthing up Celery*

intervals. The roots should be moist and the leaves dry when this job is done. Hold or tie the stems with raffia, so that the soil does not enter the centre of the plants. The leaves should be left exposed and the soil made smooth and steep, so that rain drains away. The blanching process takes seven or eight weeks. During severe frosts celery plants should be protected by straw, bracken or similar material, removing it during mild conditions.

Blanching can also be achieved by wrapping brown or corrugated paper around the plants, tying it with raffia so that water does not remain inside.

*Celeriac*

*Varieties.* White: Bibby's Defiance, Exhibition White, Invincible, Prizetaker and Sandringham Dwarf White. Pink or red: Exhibition Red, Clayworth Prize Red and Standard bearer.

**Celery Self-Blanching.** Although not difficult to cultivate this crop demands soil rich in organic matter. If available, work farmyard manure into the ground some months before planting. Failing manure, use bulky organic material such as ripe compost, peat, leaf mould, etc., with good sprinkling of bone meal.

Apart from open ground culture, self-blanching celery can be grown where a modified form of French gardening is practiced. On suitable, well manured soils, hot bed frames can be used effectively for this celery which can follow early carrots. All that is needed is to dig and clean the ground, adding a good sprinkling of balanced organic fertiliser, or hoof and horn manure.

Do not sow seed until early spring, earlier sowings being liable to run to seed. The fine seed needs sowing thinly. The lightest possible covering of finely sifted soil is sufficient. Afterwards, water with a fine rosed can. Germination is often slow, largely depending on the temperature.

Once growth is seen, ventilation should be given and early pricking out 5 to 8 cm. apart is essential. Later move them to the open ground or frames allowing 23 cm. each way.

The basic cultural operations are hoeing, weeding, watering, blight control and sometimes help with blanching.

The close planting suggested leads to blanched stems but further help can be obtained by placing clean, dry straw between the rows ten days before the crop is gathered, which it must be prior to severe frosts. Self-blanching celery is available in early autumn before ordinary celery is ready.

Apart from the Golden Self-blanching varieties, Lathom Self-Blanching produces crisp, yellow sticks of nutty flavour, while Greensnap has light green solid, crisp heads of fine taste.

**Celeriac.** *Apium graveolens rapaceum.* The turnip-rooted or knob celery has the same flavour as that subject, with an extra nuttiness. Splendid for winter use it can be grown where celery has proved difficult to cultivate.

Celeriac is planted on the flat which means less work than is needed by celery. Best results come where an open sunny position is provided. Move the ground deeply during the winter adding farmyard manure or compost. Leave the surface rough for the weather to break down and apply a dusting of lime.

Sow seeds in a light compost in a cool greenhouse or closed frame where the temperature is about 15°C. Keep the compost moist to prevent a check. Subsequently harden off gradually, before planting out in spring.

It is helpful if mature compost or peat is worked into the bed. Alternatively, 3 or 4 oz. of hoof and horn meal to the square yard will be beneficial. Space the plants 30 to 38 cm. apart with 45 cm. between rows. Plant so the little bulbous-like roots just rest on the top of the soil. Remove side-shoots and make sure there is no shortage of moisture.

Excepting in cold districts where the roots should be stored in boxes of sand in a shed, this crop can be lifted as required. During the winter a covering of straw or bracken will be helpful. As a protection against early frosts the plants can be lightly earthed up. Celeriac can be shredded or grated and eaten raw in salads or boiled like other root crops.

*Varieties.* Giant Prague, hardy; Early Erfurt, a smaller, earlier variety and Globus of good flavour and cooking qualities.

**Celtuce.** This is an unusual vegetable but quite easy to grow. It should be sown in spring covering the seeds with 12 mm. of fine soil and allowing 30 cm. between the rows. It is advisable to sow little and often and to thin the plants so they finally stand 23 to 25 cm. apart.

This subject is sometimes referred to as the 'two in one' vegetable since the leaves can be used as lettuce and have a high vitamin content, whilst the heart or central stem is crisp with a nutty flavour, and is often eaten raw in salads or cooked in the same way as celery.

**Chicory.** *Cichorium intybus.* This subject is often thought of as something that is mixed with coffee. It is the Magdeburg Chicory which, after drying, roasting and grinding, is used for this purpose. For providing a delicious salading in winter and spring, the Brussels Witloof Chicory should be grown. This becomes available when lettuce and endive are

*Chicory*

usually scarce and expensive to buy. It can also be eaten like celery with cheese and can be stewed and served with melted butter in the same way as seakale.

*Chicory, Sugar Loaf. Producing solid heads which remain in good condition for a long time.*

*Chinese Cabbage*

showing through the soil. Keep them out of the light or they will turn green and become bitter and useless.

Another method is to cut off the leaves to within 25 mm. of the crown in the autumn. Then earth up as for celery. Supplies of delicious heads will then be available during the winter.

A fairly new variety Sugar Loaf, (Pain de Sucre) can be strongly recommended. This has the appearance of well grown cos lettuce with a long standing head most useful for salading. Red Verona is another uncommon variety, which when forced, produces a compact red head.

**Chinese Cabbage.** *Brassica chinensis.* This is more like a cos lettuce than a cabbage, with shiny green leaves forming an oval or oblong head. Used in China for many centuries, it is only since the beginning of the present one that it has attracted attention in other countries having first gained notoriety in the United States.

The plants must be used immediately they mature otherwise they throw up flower heads

Sow in spring in rows 45 cm. apart, thinning the seedlings so there are 30 cm. between them. A well worked soil plentifully supplied with organic matter which does not dry out should be selected.

Forcing begins in succession in October when roots are lifted from the open ground. The best roots for forcing are about 40 mm. in diameter. Chicory can be forwarded in sheds, but a cool or cold greenhouse is better.

The procedure is simple. Make a trench 30 cm. deep and 60 cm. wide, fork the bottom and place the roots upright and close together. When the trench is full of roots water should be given. Soil from the second trench can be used to cover the roots in the first trench. A good watering will wash the soil around the roots. Then place the remainder of the soil over the roots to a depth of 23 to 25 cm. The last soil covering must be dry to ensure clean, healthy heads. Chicory is ready for cutting when the tops, known as chicons, start

*Chinese Cabbage. Can be eaten raw in salads or cooked. Midribs can be served like asparagus.*

and become useless. Frosts will spoil the plants. In hot weather, if the soil becomes dry, the leaves are inclined to wilt badly and soon lose their freshness.

Sow at intervals throughout the summer, making the drills 60 cm. apart and 25 mm. deep, thinning the seedlings so there are 23 cm. between them. Chinese cabbages do not transplant well and are at their best during a damp season.

As the heads develop, a tie or two of raffia should be placed around the outer leaves to ensure the formation of a good blanched head. The heads are cut complete as with cabbage. The leaves can be used as a substitute for lettuce or steamed or boiled. There is no unpleasant cabbage smell when they are cooked.

*Varieties.* Chili, tender, crisp, spicy flavour. Pte sai. Pure white, cos lettuce-like heads when blanched. Michikli. Growing 38 to 45 cm. tall, and up to 7 to 10 cm. in diameter. Wong Bok, large, tender, juicy heads.

**Chinese Mustard.** Widely used in the United States and parts of North America and some-times available in tins or cans, Chinese Mustard is not unlike the better known Chinese Cab-bage, its loose, rather open habit of growth making it distinct. It is hardy and has the value of resisting hot, dry weather being available when many other forms of 'greens' fail to grow well and are in short supply.

Growing about 60 cm. high, it has several common names including mustard greens, mustard spinach and tender greens, and it is sometimes used as a substitute for spinach.

Seed can be sown during spring and summer, making the rows 38 cm. apart and thinning the seedlings so there is about 15 cm. between them. In fairly rich, moist soil, growth is rapid and it is often possible to gather leaves within seven or eight weeks of sowing.

The plants must not be left unused however, or they will quickly run to seed. It is advisable to cut the entire plant at ground level rather than picking off individual leaves as is done with spinach.

If the ground is on the poor side, it should be enriched before planting and when in growth, the plants can be encouraged to make more leaves by applying dried blood fertiliser.

**Chives.** *Allium schoenoprasum.* This is a minia-ture growing onion often used as a substitute for the well known spring onion. It is largely grown for its grass-like foliage which can be cut and used to flavour salads, soups and other dishes.

It is possible to buy plants from nurserymen in the spring and these should be planted 20 to 30 cm. apart. They are sometimes used as an edging to beds in the vegetable garden. Keep the plants strong and healthy by dividing the clumps every three or four years, replanting in fresh ground.

To ensure the continued production of foliage or 'grass' the plants should be cut down to soil level from time to time whether the foliage is needed or not. This encourages plenty of young, tender shoots to develop and prevents flowering.

Chives can be raised from seed sown in spring making the drills 6 mm. deep. Thin the seedlings so they stand 15 to 20 cm. apart.

**Chopsuey Greens.** (Chrysanthemum). Al-though we would not normally think of using plants of chrysanthemums as a vegetable, in Japan and China, there are several species which are highly valued as greens. The best known of these appears to be the Chrysanthemum coro-narium varieties, which are known as Chop-suey or Shungiku. These have small, deeply cut bright green aromatic leaves.

The distinct flavour is pleasing to the taste, especially after one has become used to the idea of eating chrysanthemums.

Sow small quantities of seed in drills 30 cm. apart, at frequent intervals during spring. The greens are used when the plants are small. In normal growing weather, it is usually possible to cut shoots within six or seven weeks of sow-ing seed. When freshly gathered from plants 13 to 15 cm. high, the flavour is at its best and not too strong.

**Corn Salad.** *Valerianella olitoria* is often known as Lamb's Lettuce and there are several good improved cultivated forms.

Easily grown, it is a useful substitute for let-tuce during the winter. This crop can very well follow early potatoes, peas or broccoli and the drills should be made 18 mm. deep and 30 cm. apart.

The plants are not unlike the Forget-me-Not but without the blue flowers. An excellent

*Corn Salad*

cloche crop, it can be eaten either raw or cooked. Sowings can be made at intervals throughout the summer which will provide supplies from autumn until spring. The young plants should be thinned out so there is 15 cm. between them.

**Couve tronchuda.** Sometimes known as Portugal or Braganza Cabbage, this is a little known vegetable although it has been in cultivation for almost 150 years. One drawback is that the plants require a space of at least 75 cm. each way and so much room cannot always be spared in small gardens.

It is a kind of cabbage of which the mid-rib of the larger leaves is eaten. These, from well grown plants, are thick, white and tender. Cooked like seakale they are delicious. The green parts of the leaves and the centre heart can be used in the same way as ordinary cabbage, but need careful cooking, otherwise they are liable to be coarse and somewhat stringy.

Sow seed in spring and transplant the seedlings while they are small. A fairly rich soil on the heavy side in an unexposed position suits this crop, which should never lack moisture during the summer.

**Courgettes.** These are really very tender baby marrows which have long been popular in France.

Cooked whole and eaten with melted butter, they form a very palatable dish. There are several types now available, all being easy to grow. They include Zucchini of which the fruits are a deep emerald-green colour of attractive appearance and of excellent table quality. This variety and Cocozelle are generally reckoned to have originated from Italy.

It is possible to use bush and green trailing marrows as courgettes if the fruit is gathered when it is very small. It is however, much better to buy the special strains of courgettes rather than cut the very young fruit from the standard bush variety.

The cultural details and times of sowing and planting of courgettes, are the same as those for the ordinary vegetable marrows, using Dutch light frames.

**Cress.** *Lepidium sativum.* is the plain leaved or common cress which is easy to grow in trays or pots, or on the greenhouse bench in beds of finely sifted soil. The curled or double cress is preferred by some gardeners.

*Cress*

Seed can be sown under glass during the autumn and winter when it will provide valuable salad material while it is also in demand during the spring and summer.

*Courgette. These bushy plants produce many tender fruits which should be cooked when small.*

Known in Britain for over 400 years it was at one time valued for the medicinal properties in the seed while it has food value, since it contains vitamins c and b.1. It is also useful for green manuring.

Cress should be sown four days before mustard if both crops are to mature together. A minimum temperature of 50°C. is suitable and a fine, fairly rich nicely moist compost should be used. The seeds need only be pressed in and not covered with soil. After sowing place damp paper or hessian over the receptacles or seed beds, removing it as soon as growth is seen. This prevents the surface soil from drying out and encourages germination.

Sufficient moisture must always be available. If the compost is nicely moist at sowing time, no further watering need be done again until the seedlings are growing well.

Where small quantities are needed it is possible to sow seed directly into small punnets or pots. Seed can also be sown outdoors on prepared sites, although there is a greater possibility of grittiness. Slightly raised beds help to avoid this.

**American or Land Cress,** *Barbarea praecox,* is an excellent substitute for watercress. In spite of its name it is a native of Britain and hardly known in America. It does not require water in the same way as the normal watercress and is much easier to manage. This crop appreciates semi-shade and does well on a north border. It succeeds in town gardens and in damp situations not tolerated by other vegetables.

A seed bed having plenty of organic material should be made up. Bring the surface to a fine tilth and broadcast or sow the seed in drills 15 to 20 cm. apart. First sowings can be made in early spring to give pickings from mid-summer onwards.

Use the tender, young, leafy shoots and keep the soil moist for continued production. Seed of American or Belle Isle perennial cress, can also be sown in summer, the plants wintered under well ventilated frames for early spring pickings. Protection may be necessary during severe weather and care is needed in regard to watering.

A less common variety known as Australian

cress has pointed leaves of a mild, agreeable flavour.

**Cucumber.** *Cucumis sativus.*

A member of the Gourd family, this subject has a long history of culture, being mentioned in the Old Testament as one of the fruits the Israelites longed for while in captivity.

There are records showing that the Romans went to a lot of trouble to cultivate cucumbers, which apparently were regularly eaten by the Emperor Tiberias. The cucumber has not a high food value although it contains some vitamins C and B.

It is usual to grow cucumbers in specially prepared beds in the greenhouse. Since the roots of the plants pass through the bed and into the lower soil, the condition of the latter is of real importance. It must be kept free from disease spores, pests and injurious substances. The plants grow best when there is plenty of coarse organic material at their roots especially where this is over a well drained, gravelly or sandy but not dry subsoil. Neither a sandy or a clayey soil by itself is suitable for producing a good crop. Sterilising or steaming the base each year before the beds are made up results in better crops.

Cucumber beds can be made with good clean straw, horse manure and turfy loam, which has not been stacked too long or it will have lost a good deal of its fibre. Two parts loam to one of strawy manure are about right. Bone meal and hoof and horn, can be mixed, either with the loam, or when it has been mixed with the manure, while a 60 size potful of chalk to each barrow load of loam is beneficial.

According to heat available sow the seed from December onwards either in the 35 × 23 cm. seed trays or for small quantities one seed in each 8 cm. pot. Use a clean seed sowing mixture to ensure the absence of fungus or pests. Fill the receptacles with compost to within 13 mm. of the top and since a fairly open medium is best, the compost should not be too fine. Seeds germinate better if placed edgeways or on their sides, points downwards.

After watering, cover with glass and paper and keep them on the staging in a temperature of at least 18°C. for rapid germination is

*Apple Cucumber. Excellent for salads, very prolific.*

required and usually takes three days, the glass then being removed.

Seedlings need moving to 8 cm. pots within a fortnight of sowing. As growth proceeds, move to 12 cm. pots and later plant out in the greenhouse or frame. The night temperature should not fall below 15°C. A continuous humid atmosphere is necessary and the soil must be kept aerated. A spacing of at least 60 cm. apart is needed.

The plants require training and those in frames should have their growing point nipped out when three rough leaves have formed. The growing points of the resultant two side shoots must also be taken out.

This will give four leaders which can be trained into the corners of the frame. They in turn are stopped when they reach the limit of the space available. The lateral shoots which then develop should be stopped one leaf beyond each fruit.

Greenhouse plants need training on wires, the leaders being stopped on reaching the ridge. Fruit normally forms on the laterals which must be stopped at two leaves beyond the fruit. The female flowers are easily distinguishable by the petals being on the end of the embryonic fruits. Shading of the plants is needed in hot weather for the leaves scorch easily.

Since fertilisation reduces the cropping capacity of the plants, the male flowers should be removed unless seed is being saved. When surface roots appear top dress the soil around the plants with rich compost. In dry weather water the plants well but do not let moisture gather round the stems. Shade the glass with lime wash. Once the cucumbers are swelling nicely liquid feeds of organic liquid manure at eight to ten day intervals will be helpful. Cut the fruits before they become old. If any damp off while small, withhold water for a few days.

*Varieties* include Butchers Disease Resisting, Telegraph and Conqueror. There are, however, a number of fairly new F.1 hybrids which are most reliable, these include Fertila, and Femspot both of which do not produce male flowers and therefore the fruit is free from bitterness.

**The Cordon Cucumber.** This is a first cross remarkable for its hybrid vigour. It is capable of producing first class fruits within six or seven weeks of seed sowing. After sowing

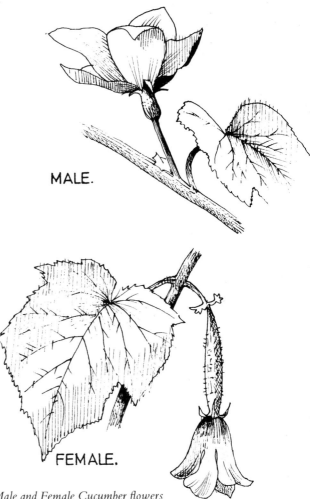

MALE.

FEMALE.

*Male and Female Cucumber flowers*

apply just enough water to dampen the seed and compost. Then place a sheet of glass on the trays or pots to prevent the soil drying out.

Germination is rapid and the seedlings must be gradually introduced to full light. Potting can be done the third day after sowing. Place the trays or pots over hot water pipes leaving a space between the pipes and trays of about 6 in. using sacks or paper to prevent heat escaping.

Prepare the fruiting quarters by adding plenty of well rotted manure or compost. Plants can be wound up string attached to overhead wires as with tomatoes, and will normally reach up to the top wires whatever their height.

Put the plants out in the greenhouse border when the first leaf has developed, spacing them 40 to 45 cm. apart with rows 70 cm. apart.

When the second rough leaf has partially formed, carefully pick out the growing point repeating it as each new leaf is made until the required height is reached.

Good cucumbers develop in about six weeks from sowing time. The crop appears in clusters and must be thinned down to reasonable numbers, especially as further clusters will appear. Following the second cluster, adventitious shoots break along the cordon growth. Some of these can be retained, stopping being done at each joint as before.

**Ridge cucumbers** should be grown in fairly rich soil. Fresh manure should be avoided. Some gardeners plant on little mounds, well rotted manure being placed at the bottom with a sprinkling of organic fertiliser added to the soil used to fill up the holes. Sow seed in spring in a warm greenhouse or frame.

Once the first leaves have developed, move the seedlings to 60 mm. pots, where they can remain until planted outdoors after frosts are over. Alternatively, seed can be sown outdoors under warm conditions. Sown earlier, the seed is liable to rot. Cloches give valuable protection in the germinating stages.

Allow 45 to 60 cm. between plants. Where several rows are being grown space them at lease 60 to 75 cm. apart. The removal of the leading shoot when about 38 cm long will encourage branching. Nip out the growing point one leaf beyond the first fruit.

Water freely in dry weather, making sure that moisture does not settle around the stems which is unlikely if the plants are growing on mounds. Keep a watch for aphids which spoil the foliage and carry mosaic virus.

*Varieties.* Apart from the older varieties such as Stockwood Ridge there are now a number of really reliable newer varieties including Burpless Green King and Burpless Tasty Green. These are particularly useful since they do not cause indigestion in the same way as other varieties. In addition there is a group of remarkable Japanese cucumbers which are of the most simple culture, these include Kyoto Three Feet, Kaga and Chinese Long Green. Two other varieties should be mentioned Burpee hybrid and Patio-pik the latter being remarkable in that in a very small area it will produce up to thirty cucumbers per plant.

Cucumber, Burpee Hybrid. *A splendid outdoor hybrid, smooth skinned.*

*Endive*

**Endive,** *Cichorium endiva.* A useful salad plant not grown as much as it deserves. An annual, belonging to the chicory family, it first became popular early in the sixteenth century. Endive resembles lettuce although the plants have to be blanched before use, otherwise they taste bitter, being useless for salads.

66

*Endive, Green Curled. Excellent for winter salads.*

This crop prefers a well drained, sandy loam with a dry subsoil. The ground need not be freshly manured or very rich, the plants growing in soils having a high humus content. Work in a good organic fetiliser such as fish meal, 3 oz. to the square metre, before sowing seed.

The earliest sowings should be made in early spring on a hot bed in heated frames or under cloches. Plant out the resultant seedlings from mid-May onwards. Outdoors, successional sowings may be made from May until early September. Space the drills 38 cm. apart and gradually thin the seedlings so there is about 30 cm. between them.

The plants will be ready for blanching about twelve weeks after sowing. This is done by tying them with raffia or covering with slates, boards, inverted flower pots with the drainage holes blocked or with rough hay or litter. Blanching takes six or seven days, and it is best to cover a few plants at a time.

Excepting in warm districts, move the later sowings to frames or cloches for blanching.

These are two distinct types of endive, curled and plain leaved. Of the former, Ruffec and Meaux are first class. The Batavian or plain leaved sort is best for winter work, since it is hardier than the curled types.

**Garlic.** *Allium sativum.* This was first introduced to European countries by the returning Crusaders of the Middle Ages. They brought it from Ascalon from which the name of our shallot is derived. Until comparatively recently only a small number of gardeners grew garlic, but this subject is gaining popularity. Though

*Garlic*

hardy, it does best in sunny, fairly sheltered positions, a light, dry soil producing the best results. Ground manured for a previous crop should be chosen, for garlic should not be grown on freshly manured soil. Wood ash and weathered soot are beneficial if raked into the surface soil just before planting.

Garlic forms a number of bulblets or cloves as they are known, being grouped together in a whitish outer skin. A well developed bulb often consists of two or three dozen individual cloves and specimens about 25 mm. in diameter are best. Planting is usually done in early spring, but in warm districts, in light well drained soil, an October and November planting gives good results.

On wet soils grow garlic in raised beds. Space the cloves 15 to 23 cm. apart with 25 to 30 cm. between each row and cover them with 25 to 40 cm. of soil. Once the leaves become yellow and wither this is a sign that the crop is ready for lifting and drying.

Always lift with a fork. If cloves are pulled out by the stem there will be injury to the neck and an easy entry for disease spores. Thoroughly dried before storing, garlic will keep well for many months.

A tiny quantity of garlic in salads brings out the flavour of the other ingredients and it is widely believed that garlic eaten in moderation, contributes to good health.

**Gherkins.** *Cucumis anglicus.* Grown for pickling, the aim should be to produce succulent fruits up to 8 cm. long. To ensure this, gather them before they become large and coarse.

General culture is the same as for cucumbers, the main difference being that plants rarely transplant satisfactorily. It is therefore best to sow seeds where they are to remain. Do this in early summer, selecting prepared enriched sites. Bulky manure or compost encourages a good root system. Place the seed 25 mm. deep and if two are put in stations 60 cm. apart the weakest seedling can be removed when the plants are growing well.

*Varieties.* Boston Pickling is one of the finest, producing good coloured juicy fruit. Small Paris is also good. Others, chiefly of American origin, include Model, Snow's Pickling, Ohio and White Wonder, the colour referring to the spines.

*Horse-radish*

**Horse-radish.** *Armoracia rusticana* (or *Cochlearia armoracia*). A native of south-eastern Europe, although now naturalised in parts of Britain and other countries.

To secure good thick roots, it is advisable to grow it on well prepared, deeply moved and manured ground where lime is not lacking.

To prevent the roots spreading, which is one of the drawbacks of this crop, the base of the site where the plants are to be grown should be made very firm to stop the roots wandering. Roots planted horizontally are less likely to spread. If lifted and replanted annually each spring, horse-radish can be kept under control.

Not more than a dozen roots will be required for the average household. Good strong thongs about 20 cm. long and of pencil thickness are best. Reduce the buds to one. In early spring, holes should be bored out and roots or thongs dropped into them 25 cm.

apart and so that about 10 cm. of soil covers the top.

Lifted roots can be stored in moist sand where they will remain firm for use as required.

**Kale or Borecole.** *Brassica oleracea acephala.* The name of borecole is said to have been given to one particular variety of kale which was once eaten by Dutch peasants or Boars and became known as Boar's Kale.

The plants are hardy standing severe weather conditions, the quality often being improved after frosts. Since they mature in late winter they are valuable when there is little other greenstuff about. Soil containing organic matter leads to the heaviest yields and lime should not be lacking, avoid badly drained positions and frost pockets.

*Borecole*

This is a crop which can follow early potatoes, peas or broad beans for which the land was well prepared. Where this is so it is not necessary to re-dig the ground, simply remove weeds and debris.

Sow seed in spring, a little earlier in colder districts. Most kales can be sown in beds in the usual way but Hungry Gap is best sown where it is to grow.

Planting distances vary according to habit of growth. For the majority, allow 45 cm. between plants with the rows 60 cm. apart. For Hungry Gap, allow 38 cm. each way.

If the central or growing point is removed in winter it will encourage side shoots. Kale should not be used too early but kept until spring when greenstuff is scarce.

*Varieties:* Dwarf Green; Tall Green; Verdura: Extra Curled Scotch; Hungry Gap—robust and valuable for its lateness and Thousand Headed. The latter is the hardiest of the plain leaved kales.

*Kohl rabi*

**Kohl Rabi.** *Brassica oleracea caulorapa.* This crop must be grown quickly otherwise it becomes tough.

It should be used when the roots are the size of a cricket ball, when they have a distinct nutty flavour so long as they are used before they become large. A good substitute where turnips fail to succeed in light soils.

The edible portion of Kohl Rabi is the knob-like growth which appears just above ground level. This, however, should not be cooked in the same way as turnips but is best peeled and sliced before being boiled or steamed, although so long as the roots are used while they are small, it is not essential to peel them. Steamed roots can be fried when they become very tasty. Although there is a purple skinned variety, it is the green form which is most widely grown because of its tenderness.

69

*Kohl Rabi. Used when small, they have a superb nutty flavour.*

Sow seed in spring, either broadcast or in drills 38 cm. apart and the roots will be ready from late summer onwards. Thin the seedlings so there is 15 cm. between them.

Kohl rabi is not particular as to soil as long as it contains plenty of humus matter and is well drained. This hardy plant normally comes through the winter unharmed although the roots will not keep for any length of time when stored.

**Leeks.** *Allium porrum.* The leek has been in cultivation for many centuries and was held in high esteem by the ancient Egyptians. Nero is said to have valued it as a voice improver. It is the national emblem of the Welsh, and as a member of the onion family is reckoned to have health promoting qualities. One reason for its popularity is that it is very hardy, which is why leeks have always found favour in colder areas.

Leeks will grow in almost all soils which are moisture retentive, without being badly drained. The plants are best grown in trenches. These should be 25 to 30 cm. deep, and 30 cm. wide, for a single row or 45 cm. wide for a double row. Work in decayed manure, compost or other organic matter, on top of which place a layer of fine soil to bring the depth of

*Leeks*

70

the trench to 15 cm. Do not use fresh manure which is liable to lead to coarse, rough growth instead of the needed tight thick stems. Where bulky manure is not available, use fish manure or bone meal, 2 or 3 oz. to the square yard.

The earliest sowing can be made in a temperature of 15 to 18°C using trays or pans of the John Innes seed compost. When the seedlings can be handled, prick them out keeping them in full light near the glass in a temperature of around 12° C. Subsequently move the plants to the cold frame for hardening off before planting outdoors in spring.

Alternatively, sow under cloches or frames in early spring and after germination the young plants can be left uncovered. Once they are 20 to 23 cm. high, move them to their final positions.

The earliest leeks can be grown on the flat. For these, make 15 cm. deep dibber holes 15 to 20 cm. apart, and drop the seedlings into them. Do not fill the holes with soil, instead, pour a little water into each hole. This will wash some soil over the roots. Fill up the holes as growth develops, although they often fill naturally from the effects of weather. If the foliage droops or if the tips of leaves wilt or lie on the soil, cut them back or worms may pull them into the soil and upset the plants.

Once they are growing well they can be helped by dusting an organic fertiliser along the rows at the rate of $1\frac{1}{2}$ to 2 oz. to the yard run. Alternatively apply liquid manure at fourteen day intervals. Keep down weeds and nip out flower stems if seen.

In trenches, the earthing up process will normally begin about a month after planting, soil being drawn up at intervals of three or four weeks. Soil used for earthing up should be fine so that the plant stems are covered evenly. Some gardeners place rings of corrugated paper around the stems before earthing up. This stops the soil from falling between the leaves and prevents grittiness when the leeks are cooked.

Very late planted leeks can be earthed up, for this speeds the blanching process. Moisture must be kept out of the centre of the plants which need regular watering, liquid manure being beneficial. Any still in the ground in the spring, should be heeled in near a north wall or hedge. This releases the ground for another crop and prevents the plants from running to seed.

For exhibition, leeks require extra cultural attention. The standard is high and 15 cm. or more, should be the length of the blanched portion of stem. Leek measurement tables are often used and competition is keen.

Wide spacing is needed for exhibition plants with some protection where the situation is exposed. Sometimes bottomless stone jars are placed over the plants. These help to increase the length of blanched stem and give protection against winds and frosts.

*Varieties* include Musselburgh, thick stems; The Lyon; Prizetaker; Broad London or American Flag and Marble Pillar, a fairly new sort producing long solid white stems. Walton Mammoth is one of the best, with long thick, solid stems valuable for exhibition. Specialist showmen often hold their own stock of which they do not disclose the origin.

**Landcress** often known as American cress, can be grown in the open ground preferably in cool, partially shaded beds. The top soil should contain plenty of organic matter so that it retains moisture.

**Lettuce.** *Lactuca sativa.* The cultivation of lettuce as a salad plant is said to date back to ancient Greek and Roman times. These plants have a wide distribution in central and southern Europe, as well as in Asia. Lettuce is largely used in salads, and is valued because of its protective food content. It is the outer leaves which are of the most value and not the inner or blanched leaves, which so often are the most highly regarded.

Lettuce is divided into two main sections, cabbage and cos, the former being the most widely grown. There are many types of these, the so-called butter varieties, with their soft lightish green leaves being most in demand.

There are varieties suitable for winter and summer production, some being quite large, others, such as Tom Thumb, making small specimens. Many varieties can be grown under heated or cold glass, in greenhouses or frames. By proper management it is possible to have fresh lettuce available throughout the year.

Although an easy crop to grow, it is important to provide sufficient moisture, particularly

*Lettuce, Little Gem. Medium sized, crisp and hearting well, superb flavour.*

*Lettuce, Fortune. A quick growing Butterhead variety.*

for summer varieties. Avoid dry soil for this can cause plants to bolt. Ideally, a cool well-drained medium loam is best, with a fairly high water-table. Plenty of organic matter if forked into the soil during the early preparation will be helpful.

Fresh manure should be avoided although really decayed matter, compost, in fact anything which will add bulk, will be of great help in getting the soil into a condition for the promotion of fibrous roots. A dressing of fish manure, 3 oz. to the square yard, well worked in will ensure that feeding material is available. If there is lack of lime, a dusting previous to sowing will be of benefit.

It is best to sow summer lettuce where they are to mature. The earliest sowings can be made towards the end of March, although there is no point in doing so in very cold districts or when the soil is wet. It is better to sow a little seed at frequent intervals rather than large quantities at any one time.

Make the drills about 25 mm deep with at least 30 cm. between them, and cover the seed with fine soil. Thin sowing should be practiced, so that there is little necessity of thinning the rows.

It is a good plan to use some of the plants

before they grow too large. This prevents overcrowding, which because of root competition can sometimes lead to bolting. Weeds must be kept down.

Winter lettuce can be sown in light well-drained soil. If the plants can follow a crop which was well manured this should encourage steady growth. Here again, if some good organic fertiliser is worked into the surface soil, at the rate of 3 oz. to the square yard, it will be helpful.

Seed of winter lettuce should be sown in late summer making the rows 30 cm. apart and thinning the plants out early so that there is about 13 cm. between them. Thin the rows later, every alternate plant being removed, and although these plants will not have formed a real heart, they can be used in the kitchen. Winter lettuce can also be sown in pots or boxes; in fact, this may be necessary in cold and northern areas. Seedlings raised in this way will be ready for planting out in October according to soil situation and district. It is of course, possible to leave the lettuce in seed beds to over-winter, the plants being put out in March. They will then be ready for use later in the spring.

When heat is available lettuce can become

*Lettuce, Minetto. Producing well folded, crisp, tender heads.*

a really profitable crop. There are certain varieties which have been bred for production under glass in winter. With all of these, plenty of light is essential and this is one reason why it is necessary to keep the glass clean. An important part of the growing process of lettuce is the raising of the seedlings. If a properly made compost is used there should be no trouble from botrytis infection.

Sow the seed in the standard size trays and if carefully done, 150 seeds will be sufficient for each tray. The seedlings can be planted into their final cropping places as soon as they are well developed and the first pair of true leaves are showing.

Final spacing varies according to variety, some sorts growing larger than others. Even the largest varieties should not need more than 23 cm. each way, and many are placed in rows 18 to 20 cm. apart, with 18 cm. between plants.

Once the greenhouse or frames are filled it is a good plan to water them well straight away and to maintain a temperature of just over 15°C. After about ten days the temperature can be lowered to 10°C. or so. Little more water will be necessary until they are established after which time it will need to be given much

*Lettuces, Vanguard and Vanmax. Late varieties of good eating quality.*

more freely.

When planting out seedlings, whether in the open ground or in greenhouses make sure the tap root goes straight down and is not turned up in the hole.

Lettuce sometimes bolt or run to seed prematurely. This condition is often caused by dry growing conditions and by the check of transplanting especially if the roots are broken.

Lettuces are ready for gathering as soon as the heart is nicely solid. Once growth begins to push up from the centre, it is a sign that the plants are beginning to run to seed and they should therefore be moved as soon as possible. If it is not possible to use them immediately they can be pulled up completely with roots and placed in a cool, shaded position in vessels of very shallow water.

The majority of the best modern varieties of cos lettuces are self-folding and need no help by tying. Even so, during spells of dry weather they may not heart up well, and it is a good plan to give a light tying with raffia, soft string, or to use a rubber band although the latter sometimes cut into the leaves rather badly.

There are some varieties of lettuces, chiefly of American origin, which do not heart, and in these cases individual leaves can be pulled off and used as required. Notable among these is Salad Bowl which is shaped like a large flat rosette, about a foot across, with curled and fimbriated leaves.

As a result of international comparison trials the number of lettuce varieties in general cultivation has recently been reduced but there are still many sorts offered in seedsmen's catalogues. They are usually grouped under separate headings which give an indication of their type.

*Crisphead or Butterhead:* Avoncrisp, Buttercrunch, Great Lakes, Iceburg, Kwiek, Tom Thumb, Webb's Wonderful.

*Loosehead sorts:* Grand Rapids, Salad Bowl.

*Cos Lettuce:* Little Gem, Paris White.

*Hardy Winter Lettuce:* Arctic King, Imperial and Valdor.

*Forcing varieties:* Kordaat, Kloek, May Queen and Premier, all of these being excellent for sowing under glass in the autumn.

**Melon.** *Cucumis melo.* These plants have been in cultivation for centuries. They are easy to manage when grown in favourable positions and where they have the maximum amount of sunshine.

Sow seed in heated frames in spring or on hotbeds of about 22°C using pots or boxes. A mixture of loam and peat is suitable, a little wood ash and old mortar rubble being useful additions.

Place the seed edgeways, 12 mm. deep, and keep the frames closed until germination occurs. Then give ventilation and water as necessary. When the seedlings have two leaves, move them to the frame or Dutch light where a hotbed has been prepared. Handle them with care and give shade until they are established.

Collar Rot and root rot are sometimes a trouble. It is an advantage to plant on slightly raised soil to prevent moisture collecting around the base of the stem at soil level. Shade from direct sunshine and regular ventilation are important factors in culture.

Frequent syringings of water help to provide a moist atmosphere. When the plants have formed three leaves, pinch out the leading shoot preferably when it is sunny, to encourage quick healing. Once the laterals have formed four leaves, they too are stopped above the third leaf. It is on the sublaterals that the fruit is borne.

Plants produce male and female flowers, the latter being recognised by a small swelling at the base. The male pollen bearing flowers, are smaller. Pollen has to be transferred to the female flower. This is often done by bees but early in the season and with frame plants, it is advisable to hand pollinate. Do this by picking the male flower and lightly rubbing the pollen on to the stigma in the centre of the female flower.

The best time for this job is between 12 noon and 2 p.m. preferably when it is sunny. Then the flowers are fully open and are dry. After a few days, the swelling at the back of each female flower will begin to enlarge. When the fruitlets are the size of a walnut, select the best and cut off the remainder at one leaf above the fruit.

When of good size the plants can be placed in the cold frame or under cloches. Prepare a good hole for each plant, filling it with well rotted manure. Plant the melon on a little ridge to avoid the roots becoming waterlogged.

Signs of ripening are a crack on the fruit stalk, deeper colour and a real melon smell.

The group known as Cantaloupe, *Cucumis*

*melo reticulatus* melons are the easiest to manage. These include Dutch Net and Tiger. For growing with little or no heat, there is No Name, (strange title!) also the F.1 hybrid, Burpee Hybrid, which has rounded golden, netted fruit and thick juicy, orange flesh. It does well in frames or under cloches. Charantais is a small delicious variety, with scented flesh. Melon varieties needing heated or warm greenhouse treatment include King George, Hero of Lockinge, Superlative and the green fleshed Emerald Gem.

**Water Melons** can be grown where a little heat is available, while they are hardy enough for frame and cloche cultivation.

With heat, they can be grown in the same way as the Cantaloupes. Without warmth, sow the seed in spring using pots of peaty compost standing them in the cold frame. When the seedlings are ready for their fruiting positions select sandy soil, well mulched with good compost. Set the plants on little mounds about 75 cm. apart remembering that the plants will not be bushy specimens but will be kept to one main stem growing 1·50 m. or more. Make sure water does not settle round the plants or stem rot will develop.

Shallow furrows can be made both sides of the plants. These can be flooded as necessary during the summer or clay pots can be sunk in the soil near the plants and these can be frequently filled with water. After the fruits have set, carefully place them on pieces of asbestos or something similar to prevent slug or other pest damage.

Water melons are ready for cutting when the tendrils near the ripening fruits become dry and shrivelled. Florida Favourite is a good variety, the oval fruits of six pounds or more, having green skin and pink flesh.

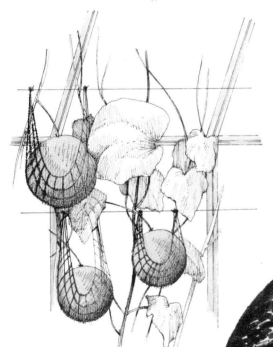

*Greenhouse melons supported in loose netting bags*

*Melon*

**Mung Beans.** Often known as Chinese Bean Sprouts this crop is now becoming popular because of its good food value. It has a high protein content and contains vitamin E. The tasty sprouts are often served in Chinese restaurants frequently being added to rice dishes. All they need is to be cooked for a few minutes in boiling water containing a little salt.

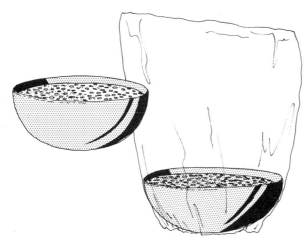

*Growing young beans indoors*

They are equally as easy to grow as mustard and cress and are most useful for persons living in a flat or otherwise without a garden. Simply sow the beans on the surface of damp peat or flannel in a dish or bowl, when they will soon germinate. Cover the containers with polythene and place them in a cupboard or other dark, moderately warm place. There, they will produce their succulent blanched top growth which will be ready for use within a few days of being sown. Cut the shoots when about 50 mm. long and cook as soon as possible when they will be crisp and nutty. Remember to keep the material moist at all times. It is best to sow small quantities at frequent intervals but these beans cannot be grown outdoors.

**Mustard.** *Brassica alba.* Hirta. White mustard is a member of the cabbage family and best known for its part in 'mustard and cress'. It is an annual plant and a native of Britain.

*Brassica sinapoioides nigra.* Black or brown mustard is not really suitable for salad purposes, since the leaves are so hot and unpalatable. In the Eastern world black mustard grows to tree-like proportions.

*Brassica nepus* or Rape is often used instead of white mustard for salad purposes. Its leaves maintain their colour well and do not decay so quickly as mustard—an important point.

The culture of white mustard or rape is exactly the same as for cress. Sow in a temperature of not less than 10°C otherwise growth will be poor. Too much heat causes the leaves to become limp and thin. Mustard can be grown in the greenhouse, frame or under cloches.

Grown in the open, the foliage is liable to become gritty and beaten down by heavy rains. The aim should be to sow regularly and often and three days after cress if it is intended that both crops should mature together. For a square yard of mustard about $\frac{1}{2}$ lb. of seed is needed.

*Mustard*

**Nasturtium.** *Tropaeolum majus.* Although well known as a flowering ornamental subject, the nasturtium is also of value as a salad plant. The leaves used when young and clean provide a piquancy which might otherwise be lacking, while the seeds can also be included in the salad bowl although they are rather hot. Not only are the flowers ornamental, but they can be eaten and seen arranged with other ingredients they provide a really bright and appetising display.

Nasturtiums grow well on any ordinary, even poor soil. If given really good treatment they are apt to produce leafy growth at the expense of flowers. The large seeds can be sown individually 12 mm. deep. Watch the plants

*Nasturtium*

weather. Where a heated greenhouse is available, seed can be sown in winter using boxes of fine nicely moist compost, lightly pressed down. Gradually harden off the seedlings for planting outdoors in early spring. Outdoor sowings in really fertile soil should be made in spring. Thin the seedlings well making sure to re-firm the soil.

Some growers leave the drills open until the seed begins to germinate. This enables the seed cases to be thrown off easily. As soon as the seedlings are developing well, and have made three or four leaves, they can be pricked out. This is done after they are hardened off.

The bed should then be trodden over again to make it firm, all stones, lumps, rubbish, etc., being removed. It is best to use a trowel so that the roots can go straignt down. The base of the seedlings should be about 2 cm. below the sur-

for aphis since these pests can soon make the plants look unsightly. A derris based insecticide will get rid of this trouble.

There are many separate named sorts as well as mixtures and it is best to depend on the dwarfer bushy strains rather than the trailing or climbing forms.

**Onions.** *Allium cepa.* These require a long season of growth and soil preparation should start in the autumn or early in the New Year particularly for exhibition purposes. A first sowing can be made in late summer or early autumn choosing a sheltered border. If it is not in good condition add a dressing of well decayed manure. Move the soil deeply tread it over to make it firm and raking it to remove any lumps.

Draw out drills 30 to 38 cm. apart and up to 2 cm. deep and in these sow the seed evenly. Lightly cover it with fine soil and then give a light treading over the drills and rake level.

If cloches are employed these will be very useful in giving protection during severe

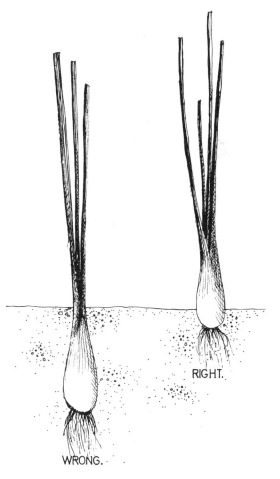

*Planting Onions*

77

face. Onions vary greatly in size, colour, shape and keeping qualities. Where specially large onions are required for exhibition, space the seedlings about 25 to 30 cm. apart.

*Varieties.* Ailsa Craig, Bedfordshire Champion, Flagon, James' Keeping, Prizetaker, Reliance, (syn. Big Boy or Okay), Up-to-Date, Premier, Rousham Park Hero and White Spanish. For pickling use The Queen, Silver-Skinned Pickling or Barletta Barla, the latter being early maturing. The best variety for spring or salad onions is White Lisbon which should be sown thickly in spring or autumn.

Onion sets have been used during recent years and are useful where it is difficult to raise onions from seed. Planting is done in spring in shallow drills 30 cm. apart and 2 cm. deep. There are now several varieties available the best known being Stuttgarter Giant. Stuttgarter Reisen is another widely grown sort, but probably the best of all is Sturon, which is considered to be superior to other sorts. The rounded bulbs have an amber coloured skin and they grow to a very large size, the flavour being excellent.

The keeping quality of onions is largely influenced by the proper ripening and correct harvesting and drying of the bulbs. The foliage usually begins to yellow in summer and soon falls to the ground. At that time all watering and feeding should stop. Where the leaves do not topple naturally, they should be gently pulled down towards the soil.

Once the foliage is quite dead, lift the onions and lay them out to dry in a sunny position providing cover at night time. Alternatively, dry them gradually on the greenhouse staging or under cloches. Once the bulbs are really dry,

*Harvesting Onions. Bulbs must be thoroughly dried if they are to store well.*

remove the dead roots and dry skin and store in trays or if you can, rope them in the old fashioned way.

**Onions,** Japanese Bunching. This is a plant which retains its foliage throughout the winter. The leaves are excellent for flavouring, while their silvery white stems or scallions are valuable in salads. It is easily raised from seed.

**Onion Potato.** The potato or underground onion is grown chiefly in Ireland and is of value where it is difficult to produce good onions from seeds. They like well-drained soil and an open but unexposed position. Plant in spring placing them 20 to 23 cm. apart, with 30 cm. between the rows.

Cover the bulbs with 2 cm. of soil and during growth they will gradually work their way upwards. Towards the end of summer scrape the soil from the bulbs to encourage the ripening process. Before storing they must be thoroughly dried off or they will not keep well.

**Onion, Tree.** The tree or Egyptian onion is of Canadian origin, and useful where onion fly is troublesome. It grows about 1·20 m. high and, in addition to the bulbs it forms in the ground,

*Potato onion*

clusters of onions develop at the top of the stem. Valuable for pickling and flavouring, they are rather hot. Sets or bulbs can be planted in spring or autumn, placing them 25 to 30 cm. apart and 5 cm. deep. Leave them undisturbed for five years or so.

**Onions Welsh.** The Welsh onion is not Welsh at all but comes from Siberia! Very hardy, it does not form real bulbs but produces many white-based scallions or chibolds. These are used as spring onions. Sometimes known as Japanese leeks, they like a well drained position.

Plants can be raised from seed sown in spring. Thin out the seedlings in the ordinary way, spacing them 6 cm. deep and 23 to 30 cm. apart. Dig up the entire plants and separate the stems for use.

*Welsh onions*

**Orach.** *Atriplex hortensis.* This is the Mountain Spinach and there are three forms; green, white and red, all growing 1·20 m. or more high. The red variety is not out of place in the flower garden, but should not be allowed to flower there, since it seeds itself freely and can become a nuisance.

The young leaves are excellent in salads, while the older ones can be cooked like spinach. People who find the ordinary spinach indigestible can eat this type without discomfort. Seed can be sown thinly in moisture-retentive ground during spring and early summer. Make the rows 45 cm. apart, and thin the seedlings early so that there is 38 cm. between them. It is best to gather some leaves from each plant rather than stripping individual plants bare.

**Okra.** *Hibiscus esculentus.* Often known as Gumbo and popular in the U.S.A. In view of our variable summer conditions, it is advisable to start the plants under glass except in warm districts. Although they grow a metre high in warmer places, elsewhere the plants rarely exceed 38 to 45 cm. The pale yellow flowers with purple centres are followed by curious long, tapering upright seed pods, which must be eaten within a few days of maturing otherwise they become tough. The okra served in restaurants is tinned and nothing like so good as fresh pods.

It is best to sow the seed in the greenhouse, placing two or three seeds in a 13 cm. pot of sandy soil, reducing the seedlings to the strongest one. These can then be planted under cloches or in a warm situation.

**Parsley.** *Petroselinum crispum.* As far as can be ascertained this plant originated in Sardinia, which island has provided us with many valuable plants. Parsley has been in use for over 500 years and has health giving properties as well as improving the flavour of dishes.

Parsley rivals mint for popularity in shops, markets and the kitchen. There are several types although the most widely grown are the numerous curled or fern-leaved varieties and the broad or plain leaved sorts. Freshly gathered parsley is best, for dried specimens are poor, unless dried quickly.

With the aid of cloches and cold frames, it is possible to have sprigs available for cutting all the year round. Seed is usually sown in succession, the first being made early in the year.

For summer use, spring sowings are the most useful, while for plants to stand the winter, sowings should be made in summer. Parsley is notoriously slow in germinating. Some gardeners pour hot water over the ground where seed has been sown.

Early thinning is essential. As a rule, plants are of little value after the second year and are best discarded, a fresh sowing being made annually.

Parsley succeeds in well cultivated soil not lacking in humus materials. Make the rows 38 to 45 cm. apart, and thin the seedlings so there is 15 cm. between them.

There are very many superstitions connected with parsley, and some people consider it unlucky to give away the roots.

**Hamburg Parsley.** *Carum petroselinum fusi-*

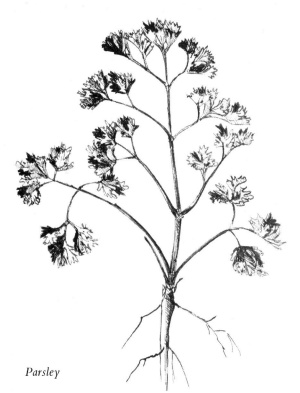

*Parsley*

*Parsley, Hamburg. Parsnip-shaped, edible roots. Foliage can be used for flavouring.*

*Hamburg Parsley*

**Parsnip.** *Pastinaca sativa.* A native of Europe, this is one of the easiest vegetables to grow. While not so popular as the potato, it is a useful winter vegetable, for steamed or baked roots can be a real delicacy. They contain vitamin C as well as some vitamins A and B1 while there are also traces of iron and calcium.

They grow best in a deep, light to medium soil not lacking in lime. Parsnips can also be grown on fairly shallow ground so long as the short rooted varieties are used. Select a site which was well manured for a previous crop. If soil is very poor and it is not possible to obtain bulky organic manure, a complete fertiliser can be used at the rate of 4 oz. per square yard.

Parsnips occupy the ground for a long time. It is often possible to sow at the end of February or early in March when soil and weather conditions are reasonable. Drills should be drawn in the usual way or a few seeds can be placed at stations 23 cm. apart. If extra large roots are

*formis*. This is a dual purpose vegetable, the roots being used like parsnips or carrots and the tops as parsley. This is not surprising when one remembers that parsley belongs to the same family as the carrot.

As the name suggests, this crop is much used in Germany where it is sometimes known as 'Jews root'.

Sow the seed in deeply cultivated ground throughout the spring. Make the drills 6 mm. deep and 38 cm. apart. Thin out the plants which grow 38 to 45 cm. high, so that there is 23 cm. between them. They like plenty of moisture during the growing season and should be kept free from weeds.

The roots can be used from early autumn. They are hardy and can be lifted as required or taken up and stored in boxes of moist sand. Well grown the roots will be 15 to 18 cm. long and look much like parsnips, but should not be peeled before using. Excellent grated raw and used in mixed salads, they should be grated just before use, otherwise they turn a light brown colour.

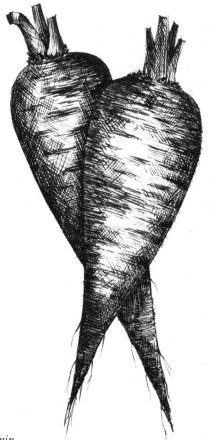

*Parsnip*

81

*Parsnip, White Gem. Fine white smooth skin –*
*resistant to canker.*

required an even wider spacing can be allowed.

Individual holes can be made up to 60 cm. deep with 8 to 12 cm. diameter at the top. Such holes can be filled with a mixture of three parts good garden soil and one part of mature compost or rotted manure. Pass these through a 7 mm. sieve. Three seeds are then sown in each hole and the seedlings thinned down to the strongest one. The drills should be 38 cm. apart.

Since the seed is liable to be slow in germinating, it is a good plan to sow radish or lettuce seed along the rows. The quick germination of these will show where the rows are, and prevent loss when the ground is being cultivated. Thinning must be done early, the best time being when the first two true leaves have developed.

The roots can be left in the soil throughout winter, and dug as required. Since they are needed during the time when the soil is liable to become frozen hard, it is a good plan to place straw or bracken around some roots, making it easy to lift them, when the soil would otherwise be frost-bound. Roots can also be lifted and stored in heaps of sand or soil or in a shed, for use during bad weather.

Parsnips are not greatly affected by any disease or pest attacks, although canker sometimes arises. This causes cracks and brown areas chiefly around the top. It is not a disease but a physiological disorder, usually caused by wet conditions, bad drainage or too much nitrogen, although hoe damage will sometimes start it.

*Varieties.* Hollow Crowned; heavy-cropping, well shaped, broad shoulders. Offenham; intermediate size, with broad shoulders, useful for shallow soils. Tender and True; medium size, extra tender flesh. The Student; well-shaped roots of fine flavour. Avonresister; having short, thick roots specially suitable for

*A good row of Peas. The result of the right cultivation.*

*Pea, Lud. Producing in pairs, pods packed with sweetly flavoured peas.*

shallow soils, resistant to rust or canker. White Gem; a new variety tolerant to canker, and a heavy cropper of medium sized roots.

**Peas.** *Pisum sativum hortense.* The garden pea has been known as a cultivated plant for centuries. Its food value is good, for among other properties peas contain vitamins A, B and C, and calcium and iron in small quantities.

Peas are grouped as either round or wrinkled. The former are hardier and are widely used for autumn sowing. Wrinkled peas are of superior flavour, but not always so heavy cropping as the round-seeded sorts. The most suitable soil is a medium loam with a fairly high water table and an adequate lime content.

The average family of four needs about 2 lb. of shelled peas to make a decent dish. In order to obtain this quantity a row about 3 m. long is required. Each row can, and should, give about four pickings, early varieties giving a little less, and the late and main crop varieties

slightly more. By careful planning it is possible to have a supply of fresh peas from the garden from late spring to early autumn.

For this five half pints of different varieties are needed, each sowing requiring about $\frac{1}{4}$ pint of seed, and ideally nine separate sowings are needed if an abundance of peas are required over a long period. The fifth sowing, can be a half pint instead of a quarter. Cloches are a help if not essential for the first three sowings, and also for the last sowing, since that crop will mature in early autumn, when often the weather becomes cold and unless covered, the crop will suffer.

Although peas obtain nitrogen from the air through root nodules, some nitrogen in the feeding given to the soil will be helpful. Where this is considered necessary dried blood can be watered in between the rows once the plants are growing nicely. Where possible peas should not be grown in the same plot more

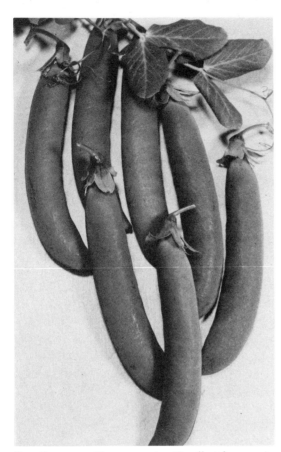

*Pea, Sweetness. Heavy cropping. Excellent for showing and for freezing.*

summer onwards, using the round-seeded varieties. The earliest spring sowings are made rather more thickly and $\frac{3}{4}$ pt. of seed will sow a row 15 m. long. For the second early and main crop varieties, about $\frac{1}{2}$ pt. will be needed. It is best to go back to the earliest wrinkled varieties for the summer sowings.

Birds often attack pea seedlings as they begin to come through the ground. It is a good plan to place pea guards or to stretch strands of black cotton along the rows. Twiggy sticks should be inserted along the rows as soon as the seedlings can be seen. This applies whether the usual pea

than once in three or four years. Rotational cropping always pays.

Once the soil has been worked into a fine, friable condition, it will be ready for sowing.

Flat-bottomed or V shaped drills should be drawn out 8cm. deep.

The distance apart depends on the variety, but as a guide, the dwarf sorts growing 30 cm. high should be allowed 60 or 90 cm. between rows, and for the taller sorts allow about the same distance between the rows as the height of the variety.

Autumn sowings must be given lighter ground. Early preparation is advisable the soil being well supplied with organic matter. Fresh manure should be avoided, since it leads to coarse growth with a poor yield of pods. Decayed manure, compost, etc. should always be worked in. Some gardeners make trenches for the rows.

Autumn sowings can be made from late

*Sowing Peas*

84

*Short twiggy supports are placed to the peas, to give them a climbing start, then taller stakes according to the normal height of the variety*

sticks or netting are to be used for the final supports. Such action will keep the seedlings from wind damage and from falling over on the ground where they become a prey to soil pests. A mulch of peat drawn towards the plants will prevent the soil drying out and ensure an even supply of moisture being available to the roots.

Earliest varieties will be ready from early summer and successional sowings will give pickings well into autumn.

*Varieties.* First Early: Early Onward 60 cm. a popular and heavy cropping sort; Feltham First 45 cm. for sowing in autumn and spring; Histon Mini 30 cm. a distinct variety early and hardy, well filled pods; Gradus 90 cm. a fine wrinkled variety; Kelvedon Wonder 45 cm. popular for spring and summer sowing; Little Marvel 45 cm. well filled pods; Meteor 45 cm. round seeded, early, for autumn or spring sowing; Pilot 1·5 m. a fine round seeded sort for early sowing.

*Second Early:* Achievement 1·20 to 1·50 m. excellent for show purposes; Green Shaft 75 cm. excellent flavour; Histon Kingsize 1·5 m. very large well filled pods; Kwartella 60 cm. an immense cropper; Recette 60 cm. a wrinkled seeded double podded variety; Victory Freezer 75 cm. vigorous growing.

*Main Crop:* Alderman 1·35 to 1·50 m. a prolific cropper; Lord Chancellor 90 cm. exceptionally heavy cropper.

*Late:* Autocrat 1·20 m. dark green pods.

**Pea, Asparagus.** *Lotus tetraglobus purpureus.* In spite of its common name it is not a normal garden pea and it is only because of its flavour that asparagus comes into the name at all. The flowers are brownish-red.

Not fully hardy it is best to raise plants in gentle heat sowing in spring, gradually harden-

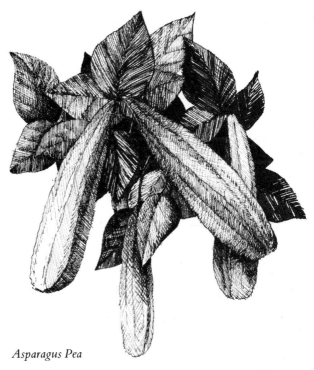

*Asparagus Pea*

85

ing off the seedlings for planting out after the frosts. Seed can also be sown outdoors where the soil is on the light side. Pick the pods while they are small—not more than 25 mm. long and cook them whole.

**Pea, Carlin.** This is a pea grown chiefly in the North of England, being used especially on mid-Lent Sunday which was once widely known as Carlin Sunday. The seeds are very distinct, being darker than any other variety.

The cultivation of the Carlin pea is the same as for the ordinary types the seed being sown in spring. Plants grow 1·80 to 2·10 m. high, and must be provided with suitable supports. Neither birds nor mice are interested in these peas, which are rarely if ever attacked by mildews, rusts or other troubles associated with the normal sorts.

The dried seeds should be soaked for some hours before being cooked until tender. If sprinkled with sugar and rum the flavour is superb.

**Pea Petit Pois.** This is reckoned by epicures to be one of the best of all peas. Very popular in France, where they seem to grow a number of sweeter varieties, they have a very delicious sugary flavour. Seed should be sown in spring, making the drills 25 mm. deep. Allow 10 to 15 cm. between the seeds, with the rows 90 cm. apart. Since the plants grow to 1·20 m. tall, it is an advantage to provide supports.

Gather the pods immediately they are filled, and if they are steamed without delay, the peas will readily fall out of the pods and the full flavour will be there too!

**Pea, Purple-Podded.** This is a little-grown type of pea, which has foliage, flowers and pods of a purple colour. It needs the normal culture for peas and is hardy. Growing about 1·60 m. high, it succeeds in almost all soils. The peas may be used when fresh in the ordinary way or can be dried for winter use. In either case they are of a most pleasing flavour.

**Peas, Sugar.** Provided they are gathered when young, these peas are a real delicacy. The entire pods are eaten; all the preparation they need being the topping and tailing as required for French beans. If the pods are picked when the peas are just swelling, they have a very sweet flavour.

Seed is sown in the ordinary way. Birds find the young pods attractive. It is therefore wise to cotton the rows. Slugs too, are liable to attack the plants or young pods if they are allowed to fall over and touch the ground. This is why they should be given supports at an early stage.

Several strains are available, including the Mange Tout pea, so popular on the Continent. This grows 1·20 m to 1·40 m. high. A new sugar pea known as Sweetpod bears light green, succulent pods of sweet flavour. Dwarf Sweetgreen grows only 45 cm. high and is an excellent cropper of sweet, good flavoured peas.

**Potatoes.** *Solanum tuberosum.* Potatoes will grow on all types of soil, although a deep, well drained medium loam is best. Soil has a great influence on flavour. Light and air are essential, for under stagnant, close conditions blight will spoil the crop. Heavy clay and peaty soils are said to produce 'waxy' or 'soapy' tubers, but this is not always so.

This crop is grown where ground needs to be cleaned before more particular crops are planted, but in a small garden it is questionable whether it is worth while growing main crop potatoes. These occupy the land much longer than the earlies, which can be followed by salad plants, brassicas or similar subjects.

Prepare the soil early. Work in farmyard manure, seaweed or compost when moving the ground during the winter. Leave the surface ridged if the land is heavy, so it breaks down easily at planting time. Some gardeners place decayed manure or compost along the rows at planting time, but if it is underneath the tubers the roots become more active. For main crops and even the second-early sorts, manure can be supplemented with a fertiliser such as bone meal or hoof and horn.

Medium sized tubers the size of a hen's egg and weighing about 2 oz. are best, the usual size being those which have passed through a 5 cm. riddle but will remain on a 2 cm. one.

It is best to buy fresh certified seed every year. Large tubers can be cut; this should be done lengthways, each portion having at least two strong sprouts. Cover the cut portions with a damp cloth until they can be planted.

One method of planting is to take out flat-bottom trenches about 10 cm. deep, deeper on light land. A layer of leaf mould or peat sprinkled along the opened trench helps to ensure the tubers retain good skins. Planting time will depend on where you live, the earliest plantings taking place in really mild districts according to weather conditions.

For the earlier, space the tubers 25 to 30 cm. apart with 45 to 52 cm. between the rows. Second earlies can be spaced 38 cm. apart with 75 cm. between rows. Main crops need to be 45 cm. apart with the rows 75 cm. apart.

Earthing up the plants gives protection from late frosts and keeps the haulms upright; it also prevents the new tubers from becoming exposed and turning green, when they become useless. The extra covering of soil also gives protection from blight.

Earthing up is done gradually and can be started when the stems are 8 to 10 cm. high. The ridges made should have fairly sharp, sloping sides, allowing heavy rains to drain away. Any flowers that develop should be removed as soon as seen.

Sprouting the tubers before planting is regarded as an essential part of the culture of potatoes. It encourages earliness and a heavy crop. The process consists of setting the tubers eye end uppermost, in shallow wooden trays placing them in a light, frost-proof place, in a temperature around 8°C.

Keep a watch for greenfly, which if seen should be sprayed with liquid derris. At planting time leave only two or three strong sprouts on each tuber—rub off the remainder. sprouting gives an opportunity to detect poor or diseased sets before planting time.

Potatoes can be grown successfully under black polythene without earthing up. Prepare the ground in the usual way and press the tubers lightly into the surface. Lay a sheet of polythene over the rows making cross cuts about 8 cm. long, like a plus sign above each tuber. Fix the edges of the polythene by taking out a little furrow 5 to 8 cm. deep. Cover the edges with soil making it firm by treading.

This leads to quick growth, suppression of weeds and the retention of moisture. Scatter slug bait under the polythene, for the dark, cool shelter this cover gives makes a possible hiding and breeding place for slugs.

Potatoes are ready for lifting when top growth has died down although the earliest crop is often ready while the haulm is still green. To ensure the tubers are ready for lifting, scrape away the soil and remove one or two tubers. Then lightly rub the skins. If they remain firm the tubers are ready. Keep them covered and out of the light, otherwise they will become green and of little value for eating.

New potatoes can be obtained in autumn by planting again on ground from which the first crop has been lifted. From the first lifting, select sound, shapely tubers about the size of a Victorian plum, weighing $1\frac{1}{2}$ to 2 oz.

Expose the tubers to the light and sun for two or three days before replanting. In a favourable sheltered site, turn the soil fairly deeply, digging in some organic fertiliser. Then make a trench 13 to 15 cm. deep and place the tubers 25 to 30 cm. apart with 52 cm. between rows. Suitable varieties include Arran Pilot and Home Guard. When the plants are growing well, cloches can be used with advantage.

There are now several scores of named varieties of potatoes in cultivation although some are difficult to obtain and others are rarely grown because they do not crop well, whilst there are some very new varieties which have not yet had sufficient trials to ensure their place in the list of standard sorts.

The following are all first class varieties immune to wart disease and there are of course many other varieties which will be found on reference to the catalogues of potato specialists. *First Early:* Arran Pilot; white flesh, shallow eyes, producing medium sized tubers. Home Guard; similar to Arran Pilot but yields slightly lower and is not quite such a good keeper. Di Vernon; white flesh splashed purple. A heavy cropper, good for exhibition. Ulster Prince; white, kidney shaped with shallow eyes. Ulster Chieftain; medium sized tubers. Not so heavy cropping as Arran Pilot. Ulster Premier; white fleshed variety which rarely discolours.

*Second Early:* Craigs Royal; creamy flesh often splashed pink, shallow eyes. Craigs Alliance; white flesh, heavy cropping. Ulster Dale; yellowish tinged flesh with shallow eyes. Heavy cropper. Great Scot; white flesh, rather deep eyes. Heavy cropper, but of indifferent cooking quality. Maris Peer; oval, creamy-white flesh, heavy croppers.

*Main Crop:* Majestic; tubers irregular in shape but heavy cropping. Liable to split. Redskin; round to oval tubers, skin pink, flesh pale lemon. Heavy cropping. Dr. McIntosh; white kidney, good cropper and fine for exhibition.

*Late Crop:* Golden Wonder; a russet kidney, reputed to be the finest flavoured potato of all. Not a heavy cropper but reliable

*Salad Potatoes:* Aura, Kerrebell, Himalayan Black and Fir Apple, the latter having a pink skin and lemon flesh.

*For frying:* Belle de Juillet, Blue Eigenheimer and Kipfler, one of the best, with a nutty flavour.

*Stormont Enterprise.* This is a new variety which has not yet been distributed but shows signs of being a valuable sort. A whole group of potatoes have been fairly recently introduced all with the preface of Pentland. These include —Beauty, Crown, Dell and Falcon. In addition, three other varieties likely to be of use for pro-cessing are Pentland Marble, P. Raven and P. Square. The latter showing signs of being in demand for canning purposes.

**Pumpkin.** *Cucurbita moschata.* This is a member of the marrow family and may be grown in the same way as the trailing marrows. They are easily raised from seed sown in the cool greenhouse or garden frame. Use 8 cm. pots of good compost sowing two seeds in each. If both grow remove the weakest specimen.

Alternatively, sow where the plants are to grow covering them with cloches, but watch out for slugs which seem attracted to the seedlings. Plant out into heaps of fermenting material. The flowers can be hand fertilised, and if the intention is to grow very large fruits then one should be allowed to develop on each plant. Smaller specimens can be gathered before the skin becomes iron-hard. If the aim is to secure giant pumpkins, plenty of liquid manure should be supplied over a period of weeks.

The variety usually grown is Hundredweight

*Pumpkin*

88

*Pumpkins, Big Max and Jack O'Lantern. Excellent for pies and useful for making 'lanterns.'*

which produces huge orange fruits and which has often been the subject for special Pumpkin Competitions.

**Radish.** *Raphanus sativus.* One of the easiest of crops to grow, this subject can be cultivated in the open ground, the cold frame and the cool greenhouse. An excellent catch crop, it can be grown on the sides of celery or leek trenches or between rows of lettuce or other salad plants. Some varieties are red, others white, while some are red and white. There is also a difference in shape, varying from round or globe to the half-long and fully long with a broad top. The newer varieties have done away with the belief that radishes are hot and a cause of indigestion.

Radishes do not need deep soil but the ground should be well prepared and remain nicely moist, for quick growth is required in order to secure crisp, succulent roots. Soil containing plenty of organic material is ideal since this ensures moisture retention. It is when the soil becomes dry that leafy growth is produced, with little or no bulb formation.

Do not sow the seed too thickly. While it is

*Radish*

*Radish, All Seasons White. For sowing in succession. cool white flesh.*

quite usual to spread the seed in a broadcast fashion, it is really best to sow in drills 15 cm. apart and about 12 mm. deep. Make the soil firm after sowing for loose soil rarely produces firm roots. A half ounce of seed will sow two rows 4·50 m. long.

If flea beetles have been troublesome in the garden, it is wise to dust the drills with naphthalene before the seed is sown. Thin the seedlings as early as possible so that all have an opportunity to develop properly. Pull the roots as soon as they are of usable size. Left too long, they may become hard, woody and 'hot'.

Varieties for early maturing outdoors include French Breakfast and Saxa, the latter being a small scarlet, quick maturing sort. Icicle is white, Wood's Early Frame a long variety, deep pink in colour, and Sparkler is half-red and half-white.

Winter radishes can be sown during the summer the warmer the area the later the sowing. Make the drills 23 cm. apart, the plants being thinned to 15 cm. in the rows. The roots can be left in the ground to be dug as required or they can be lifted in early winter and stored in boxes of sand, sandy soil or peat. Winter radishes can also be grown in boxes although these should be at least 20 to 23 cm. deep. For good results the roots require plenty of moisture in the growing season, otherwise they become stringy and very hot.

The variety China Rose is one of the best,

being somewhat like a very large French Breakfast. The skin is cerise-red, the flesh white and crisp. Black Spanish has black skin and white flesh and both need slicing and are not eaten whole.

A most unusual variety is the Bavarian radish which forms roots the size of a large turnip, the top growth reaching 75 to 90 cm. This is the variety one can see served in Bavarian beer halls where it is cut into spiral pieces or grated and served in salads. The decorative seed pods are an added attraction and it is said they make a useful sandwich filling if cut and used while they are green.

Although really an easy crop to grow, so often gardeners find they get plenty of top growth but small stringy roots. Few disappointments occur where seed is sown thinly on good ground never lacking in moisture, with shade from direct strong sunshine.

**Rampion.** *Campanula rapunculus.* This is a little-grown biennial plant of which seed should be sown in early Summer. When the soil is in a fine workable condition, make the drills 30 cm. apart and thin the seedlings so there is 10 to 13 cm. between them. This plant likes plenty of moisture so a semi-shaded position should be chosen. If the roots become dry, the plants are liable to run to seed prematurely.

The roots are hardy and can be dug as required, although it is wise to store a few in boxes of sandy soil in winter, so they are available should the ground be frozen at any time. The white fleshy roots are boiled and when tender, can be cut up for use in salads or be served with melted butter.

**Rhubarb.** *Rheum rhaponticum.* A native of China its history can be traced back to several thousand years B.C. Various species have taken part in the production of rhubarb as we know it today and through the course of time, the plant has been gradually improved.

An easy plant to grow it will remain productive for many years. It is a pity that rhubarb is often grown in positions which are badly drained or where the soil is poor.

Deeply move the soil since the plants make thick branching roots. If stable and farmyard manure and compost are worked in they will provide feeding material over a long period.

*Rhubarb pulling*

*Rhubarb, Swiss Chard. Long stalks of bright crimson. Decorative as well as valuable in the kitchen.*

Bone meal and wood ashes are also useful. For earliest outdoor rhubarb, a fairly sheltered position is required.

*Rhubarb*

Plant from autumn to spring when the soil is workable. Allow 90 cm. between the crowns for they increase in size and need ample room. Spread the roots fully, planting firmly, covering the crowns with 50 mm. of soil. Do not pull any stalks the first season and in subsequent years always leave some stalks on each plant.

It is best not to pull much after mid-summer excepting in the case of stalks needed for jam or wine making. Rhubarb should not be cut but gripped at the base of the stem and pulled with a jerking movement. Flower heads should always be removed. To keep the plants productive, give a dressing of manure annually. Inverted pots or boxes placed over some of the plants will provide outdoor pullings.

*Forcing rhubarb.* While it is usual to force three year old plants, rather younger specimens can be used, provided they are strong and healthy. Plants to be forced should not be pulled during the summer. This means that the energy of the plants will have been directed entirely to building up strong crowns for producing good crop when forced.

The simplest way to force rhubarb is under the heated greenhouse staging. If sacks or hessian are draped in front of the staging this will provide the necessary darkness. Should hot water pipes be under the staging, it is best to stand a sheet of asbestos or some boards in front, so that dry heat does not directly reach the rhubarb.

*Timing is important.* If the aim is to produce sticks for Christmas, forcing should commence a few weeks previously. To maintain a succession, batches of crowns must be brought in at fourteen day intervals. Make sure that the soil is nicely moist before planting.

Pack the crowns closely together, filling in the spaces between them with sandy loam, fine peat or leaf mould so that there are no air pockets. Once planted, the crowns should be given a good soaking with water. To begin with, a temperature of 8°C is adequate, but a week later it should be raised to 10°C and after a further eight to ten days to 15 to 18°C.

*Varieties include:* Prince Albert, Linnaeus and Victoria. If one or more of these are grown it will provide a natural succession of sticks for pulling from April onwards. For forcing, Champagne and Dawes Champion are good, whilst the Sutton is also reliable. It is possible to raise rhubarb from seed and Glaskin's Perpetual is one of the best for this purpose and matures quickly.

**Salad Plants.** When thinking of salads many people do not go further than lettuce, tomatoes, cucumber and radishes. This is a pity since there are many interesting, health-promoting plants which are easily grown. These add pleasing variety to a mixed salad as well as being most agreeable when used alone.

The majority are best eaten raw; one or two including endive and dandelion are bitter unless blanched, while some can be cooked. With a little planning, salad plants can be available throughout the year and there is no doubt that if more raw vegetables were used, with their higher vitamin content retained, we should be a healthier nation.

The following salad subjects and their culture are fully described elsewhere. Beetroot, celeriac, celery, chicory, chives, corn salad, cress, cucumber, dandelion, endive, lettuce, mustard, nasturtium, onion, parsley, radish and rampion.

*Savoy Cabbage, Ice Queen. Vigorous growing, high yielding and very hardy.*

**Savoy.** *Brassica olerarea bullata major.* This is a distinct member of the cabbage family developed in the French region of Savoy in the Middle Ages. It is of a more dwarf habit than the true cabbage, very hardy, with crinkled leaves. It forms a typical cabbage head with a solid heart. It is generally reckoned to be unwise to grow savoys in industrial areas since dust and soot are liable to settle on the puckered leaves, often making them inedible.

The plants like a soil containing plenty of bulky material and potash but less nitrogen, since soft growth is not needed, and most need a long growing season. Culture is exactly the same as for the ordinary cabbages. There are early, mid-season and late varieties. The earlies need sowing in spring for maturing from late autumn. Maincrops are sown in summer for winter cutting, followed by the late varieties for cutting in spring.

*Varieties.* Early: Early Drumhead, early and reliable. Best of All, first class. Savoy King, an F.1 hybrid. Mid season: Tom Thumb, forming a smaller succulent head. Ice Queen, a F.1 hybrid, hardy and uniform. Late: Omega, forming large very hardy heads. Winter King, resistant to frost.

Although often classed as a cabbage, January King produces its flattish heads throughout the winter, whilst the New January Prince, matures during autumn and early winter according to sowing dates.

**Salsify.** *Tregopogon porrifolius.* This is a biennial plant, often known as the Vegetable Oyster because of its flavour. Not at all widely grown it is much in use as a winter vegetable in France and Italy. It likes a deep moisture retentive soil on the light side, preferably one enriched with decayed manure or compost the previous season.

Sow seed in spring in drills 2 cm. deep and 30 cm. apart, and thin the seedlings to 15 to 18 cm. apart. The roots are ready for use in the autumn and may be lifted as required, being treated like parsnips. Do not damage them or they will 'bleed' and loose their nutty flavour.

If some plants are left in the ground during the winter, young top growths can be cut and cooked in spring when they have an asparagus-like flavour. The cream-coloured roots should

*Salsify Mammoth. The Vegetable Oyster; of delicate, sweet flavour.*

*Salsify*

93

be 15 to 23 cm. long and 5 cm. thick. They can be steamed or boiled in their skins, which are rubbed off, before being served with white sauce. Sandwich Island Mammoth is the best known variety.

*Scorzonera*

*Seakale*

**Scorzonera.** *Scorzonera hispanica*. Very similar to salsify, this is preferred by many because of its flavour and its help in combating various forms of indigestion. Fertile soil, free from clods or stones ensures straight roots. Sow seed in the spring in drills 25 mm. deep and 38 cm. apart. Thin the seedlings early, leaving strong plants 15 cm. apart. The plants are perfectly hardy and while roots can be stored in boxes of sand it is better to lift as required and cook without delay.

Boil or stem the roots before peeling. The black skin is not easy to remove, the best way being to rub the roots in a cloth while they are hot.

**Seakale.** *Crambe maritima*. Best results come from good sandy loam which holds moisture without becoming waterlogged. Prepare the ground in autumn, working in bulky manure.

When final soil preparations are being carried out in the spring, fork in a light dressing of an organic fertiliser such as fish manure, 2 ot 3 oz. to the square yard.

Plants can be raised from seed, although a couple of years elapse before forcing crowns are produced. Sow seeds in prepared beds in early spring, making the rows 38 to 45 cm. apart. Take out any flower beads that develop.

A quicker method of propagation is by root-cuttings. Usually known as thongs, they should be straight and clean, 15 cm. long and of pencil thickness. Cut them horizontally at the top and in a sloping angle at the bottom.

These cuttings are prepared when lifting plants for forcing. Tie them in bundles and bury them in sandy soil, either in the frame or a sheltered position outdoors until planting time in the spring, when the soil is workable. While they are buried, each root normally produces several buds, but only the strongest one should be retained. Make the rows 45 cm. apart with 30 cm. between the plants.

Seakale needs forcing, and this can be done in the open by covering the plants with pots or boxes, around which old manure should be heaped. It is also possible to blanch seakale where it is growing, by earthing up the plants, using soil that is dry, fine and friable. Best results come when the roots are taken into cellars, frames or are placed under the greenhouse

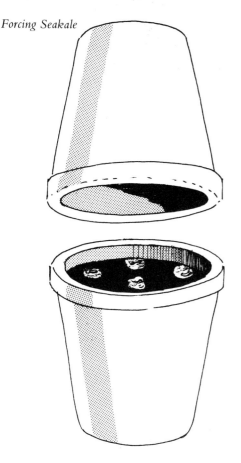

*Forcing Seakale*

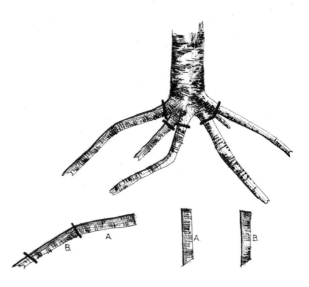

*Seakale root cuttings*

staging. Stand them upright in good soil or coarse leaf mould in complete darkness. It takes five to eight weeks according to facilities available for really good edible seakale to develop.

The heads are ready for cutting when they are about 15 to 18 cm. long and should be gathered just before they are required. If not used at once, they become of poor colour and deteriorate quickly.

Lily White is the most widely grown variety. It has pure white heads of good flavour. Ivory White is very similar.

**Seakale Beet.** *Beta vulgaris cicla.* Known under the names of Swiss Chard and Seakale Spinach, this vegetable is chiefly grown for the thick, silvery-white succulent mid-ribs which form an excellent substitute for seakale, while the remainder of the leaves can be used as spinach.

The plants flourish on most soils excepting light, quick draining ground. Best results come from prepared and manured soil. If possible dig in well rotted compost or farmyard manure in the autumn or winter, working in fish manure 2 to 3 oz. to the square yard, just before sowing the seed.

Frequent and thorough watering during dry weather will be well repaid, liquid feeds being helpful. A mulching of peat or compost prevents the surface soil drying out.

Sow throughout the spring in drills 25 mm. deep and 38 to 45 cm. apart. Thin the seedlings so there is 23 to 25 cm. between them. The leaves must be pulled off in one piece, if cut in strips, continued production is hindered and decay may set in. Keep the outer leaves picked off to encourage plenty of young tender leaves to develop.

A little lemon juice added to the water in which the mid-ribs are boiled will keep them a really clear white colour.

**Shallots.** *Allium cepa ascalonicum.* Easy to cultivate requiring the same conditions as onions, shallots grow in a wide variety of soils although they do not like heavy clay. Avoid freshly manured land, but well rotted compost or manure dug in during the autumn is beneficial, particularly where exhibition bulbs are required. Fish manure 2 to 3 oz. to the square yard is helpful.

Shallots can be raised from seed, but the plants are liable to bolt. Small bulbs are planted

*Shallots*

from early spring onwards. At one time gardeners reckoned to plant shallots on the shortest day and harvest them on the longest. This is neither necessary or practical on account of bad weather towards the end of the year.

The soil should be nicely firm at planting time. Take off loose skins and dead tops from the bulbs and press them into the soil to about half their depth. Space them 12 to 15 cm. apart with 30 cm. between rows. Slugs or birds sometimes pull the bulbs partially out of the soil and extra strong roots sometimes force them up. Inspect the roots from time to time so that loose bulbs can be pushed back into position again. Do not damage the plants when cleaning the ground.

Once the leaves turn yellow in summer, draw the soil away from the bulbs to encourage ripening. The lift and dry thoroughly before storing in a cool, dry, airy place. The red or common shallot is the most widely grown, although some gardeners like the yellow variety. Some suppliers now offer Giant Long Keeping Red and Giant Long Keeping Yellow in virus-free strains.

Classes for shallots at shows are usually closely contested. One of the most widely used varieties is Hâtive de Niort. This yields really good shaped specimens, especially if the following culture is given. A newer exhibition variety is Aristocrat which is resistant to neck rot.

The site should be prepared early, burying well rotted manure or compost one spit deep. Into the top spit, work bone meal, hoof and horn meal and bonfire ash if possible, in the ratio of three two and five.

Leave the surface soil rough, and early in the year excepting in limey soil, dust the surface with hydrated lime 4 oz. to the square yard.

Plant really sound, well-shaped, medium sized bulbs at least 25 mm. in diameter. Some specialists sprout the bulbs before planting by setting them upright in boxes of compost in the greenhouse. Plant shallowly with a trowel 30 cm. apart with 38 cm. between rows. If the rows can be covered with cloches this will ensure a quick start and prevent bird damage.

Once top growth is advancing, a few feeds of liquid manure and soot will be helpful but avoid overfeeding or the bulbs will become thick necked and will not keep.

When the foliage has turned yellow lift the bulbs with a fork and leave them to dry off under glass for a couple of days. Then clean them and place them upright in a shallow box of sand turning them occasionally so they ripen off and become an even colour. Tie down the necks and for showing, select well shaped, weighty specimens five or six to the pound.

**Skirret.** *Sium sisarum.* This old fashioned vegetable produces semi-cylindrical white roots of a pleasing distinct flavour. It is grown and used similarly to salsify. It can be raised from seed, although since it is a perennial, the tuberous roots can be divided for replacing in the spring. Once the plants begin to deteriorate a fresh supply should be obtained by sowing seed in spring.

Skirret does best in soil on the light side, and rich ground should be avoided. Roots are ready for use as required from early autumn onwards. Alternatively, the roots can be lifted in autumn and have their leaves twisted off before being stored in layers of sand or soil, either in boxes or trays kept in a cellar.

**Spinach.** *Spinacea oleracea.* Of Persian origin, this plant was once grown almost solely for medicinal purposes. There are various kinds and by careful attention to sowing times spinach can be available throughout the year. Although not everybody's favourite, this green vegetable undoubtedly has some health promoting qualities.

Summer spinach tends to run to seed quickly on light soils, so it is advisable to work into the ground bulky, moisture-holding material, decayed manure and compost being particularly

96

useful. Quick growth is needed and it is helpful to apply liquid manure along the rows once the plants are growing well. Summer spinach should be sown in very early spring, making the drills 25 mm. deep and 30 cm. apart. Cover the furrows well, firming them with the rake head. Thin seedlings early using the thinnings for salads. Make further sowings at fourteen day intervals and if the weather is very dry, first soak the seed in water for twelve hours. Once plants begin to run to seed they are best pulled up.

Winter spinach should be sown throughout mid-summer, preferably on raised well drained beds of about 8 cm. Thin the plants early so they stand 13 to 15 cm. apart.

While summer spinach can be picked quite hard, winter spinach must not be overworked. Pick outside leaves from all plants rather than stripping individual specimens. This ensures a regular supply of fresh tender leaves.

*Summer varieties:* Monstrous Viroflag. This is a fine round seeded variety with smooth round leaves. Victoria Long Standing produces thick dark green foliage. Nobel is a heavy cropper with large, fleshy leaves.

*Winter Varieties.* Giant Prickly, a hardy abundant cropper. Standwell. True to its name, hardy large succulent leaves are produced over a long period.

**Spinach Perpetual.** Spinach Beet. This is an excellent substitute for the true spinach. A perennial leaf beet, it produces green leaves but no typical beet root. The leaves are larger and more fleshy than those of summer spinach and easier to gather and cook. One sowing in spring and another in summer will usually ensure a year-round supply. On fairly rich soil make the drills 25 mm. deep and 38 cm. apart. Thin the seedlings so there is 15 to 20 cm. between them. Make sure the roots do not dry out in summer. Keep the young leaves picked even if you cannot use them immediately. Left to grow old, production slows down with loss of quality.

**Spinach. New Zealand.** *Tetragonia expansa.* Not a true spinach, this plant has similar leaves and can be used as a substitute for summer spinach. It grows well on light, dryish soils. It tolerates heat and does not run to seed like ordinary spinach. It has a different habit of growth too, since it grows rather flat on the ground. The plants do not bolt and if growing tips are kept pinched out, an abundance of leaves are produced forming a ground cover and stifling weeds.

Sow seed under glass in early spring, first soaking it in water overnight. Move plants to their final positions in late spring. Space them 60 cm. apart with 75 to 80 cm. between rows. While this spinach grows in dry soils, the leaves will be more succulent if plenty of water is given during dry weather. Alternatively, sow under cloches 'in situ' in spring. Harvesting will normally go on from mid-summer until frost kills the plants.

*Squashes*

**Squash.** Summer. *Cucurbita pepo melopepo.* Winter, *C. maxima.* These are really types of marrow and include some of the best known varieties. It is, however, the lesser known sorts that are usually meant when squashes are referred to.

Seeds can be sown in prepared stations in the open ground and if the sites are covered with cloches or jam jars, this will encourage germination. Once growth is seen, jam jars must be removed and according to weather condi-

97

tions, the plants may need covering with cloches for a week or so. When glass coverings are taken away, place brushwood among the seedlings. This gives protection from ground winds.

If slugs have been troublesome, put down slug bait. Pinch out the growing points to encourage side shoots which are the most likely to be fruitful. Hand fertilisation can be practiced, although it is usually done by wind, bees and other insects.

Make sure the plants never want for water. In naturally dry soils, it is best to prepare sites by digging 60 cm. deep holes and filling them with decayed manure, leaf mould and other humus forming, moisture holding matter. As necessary, organic liquid feeds are most helpful, but do not apply artificial fertilisers. These increase the size of the seed in the fruit.

Store the fruit in a dry, warm place. In a cold shed or cellar, the fruits lose their flavour as well as being liable to decay.

Varieties. Hubbards' Squash has green skin with yellow stripes and yellow flesh. Custard Marrow, Summer Crookneck, Giant Straightneck, Rotherside Orange and Cocozella are fine bush varieties maturing in summer. For storing in a frost proof, dry place for winter use, Butternut and Golden Delicious are first class.

*Squash. Early White Bush, Patty Pan. Grows like a marrow. Stores well.*

## Sweet Corn. *Zea mays.* Sweet corn is a distinct type of maize with a sugary fruit reserve. It is used as a vegetable and should not be confused with starchy types of maize used for fodder.

This crop is unsuited to high altitudes and places exposed to sea winds. Clay soils are unsuitable, medium and light ground being best. Land where manure was applied for a previous crop is suitable. Where really light soil has to be used, manure can be worked in before the crop goes in, while an organic fertiliser can be raked in before sowing.

Where small quantities of seed are involved, it can be sown in large 60 size pots from the second week in May onwards. It is unwise to sow before, in order to prevent the roots becoming pot bound, which causes stunting. Sowing in boxes cannot be recommended because of damage to the roots when transplanting is done.

*Sweet Corn, Golden Bantam. Medium sized, bright yellow, richly flavoured cobs.*

Seed can be sown in cold frames where the plants can be left to mature or cloches are useful for covering direct to the ground sowings.

For uncovered sowings in fine soil after frosts have passed, draw out furrows up to 5 cm. deep. Drop in two seeds at 38 cm. intervals or singly 23 to 30 cm. apart. For the latest sorts make the spacing 52 to 60 cm. apart.

Thinning is done at the five leaf stage and all unhealthy or insect attacked plants should be hoed out. Sweet corn which is wind and insect pollenated, carries male and female flowers on the same plant. Successful pollenation requires a fairly dry atmosphere. The best crops are secured where the plants are grown in blocks, because the pollen can easily reach other plants instead of being lost which nearly always happens when the plants are grown in single straight rows. In exposed gardens, the plants should be slightly earthed up. Make sure the roots do not become dry.

The grains set after fertilisation and become the edible 'cob'. Proper harvesting influences the yield and it is necessary to gather carefully so that only fully developed cobs are cut or picked. Once the green husks are pulled aside, the way is open for earwigs to enter. It is therefore, most unwise to strip off the husk to find out if the 'corn' is ready.

The cobs will ripen in succession and should be cut before the seeds become hard. If a creamy solution springs from the grains when pressed with a fingernail, they are ripe. The cobs are trimmed by removing untidy 'silk' or broken outer husks.

Keep the cobs in the cool until they are used. They can be eaten on the stalk, or by cooking the grains in a little boiling margarine, can be made into 'popcorns'.

*Varieties.* Golden Bantam, early sweet and tender. Prima, fourteen days earlier than Golden Bantam. Golden Standard, a heavy cropper, tall growing, but not so good flavour. Reliable new varieties include Kelvedon Glory and Xtra Sweet, a very early F.1 hybrid of good flavour.

**Swede** or Swede Turnip (U.S.A.). *Brassica napobrassica.* Giant Turnips, which are known as swedes, originated in Sweden more than 180 years ago. They are hybrids between a turnip and other members of the cabbage family. Hardier than turnips, swedes are sweeter but slower growing. They rarely become woody.

*Sweet corn, tassels and cobs*

*Removal of sweet corn side shoots*

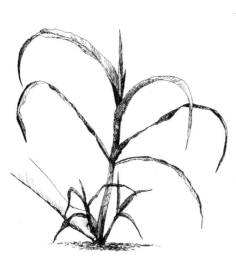

*Swede*

Sowing time is in spring according to soil and weather conditions.

Swedes prefer well drained soil, rich in organic matter and early preparation is advisable, working in famyard manure or compost. Sow in 25 mm. deep drills, 45 cm. apart, and subsequently thin the seedlings so that there is 30 cm. between them.

*Varieties.* Purple Top, Lord Derby, Tipperary and Great Scot. The latter has bronzy-green foliage.

**Turnip.** *Brassica rapa.* The wild form can sometimes be found in waste places, but named varieties are the result of plant breeding and selection. Turnips have some food value, since they contain vitamin C., calcium and iron, while turnip tops have a high vitamin B content.

Fairly sandy soil is suitable, especially since this is likely to warm up early giving a good start to the first sowings. Early and thorough preparation is advisable preferably on a site which was well fed for a previous crop. Freshly manured ground encourages the development of fanged roots.

Break down the soil well before sowing time

*Turnip*

and make sowings at fortnightly intervals. The winter types being sown the latest.

Make the rows 30 cm. apart, although if mechanical cultivation is to be employed, they may have to be from 30 to 45 cm. according to the type of cultivator used. This will naturally affect the quantity of seed required.

After sowing the soil should be made firm. Subsequently it will be necessary to hoe between rows. Once germination occurs and there is the possibility of flea beetle attacks, dust with derris or Pyrethrum powder.

Little thinning out is necessary since roots are pulled when small. Later crops can be thinned to 15 cm. apart. Turnips must not lack moisture and it is essential to keep down weeds, for if left, they compete for the moisture and food available.

*Vegetable Marrows. Securing an early crop under cloches.*

*Marrow*

While the earliest of the main crops will be ready in early autumn, roots from clamps will be available until spring. Most varieties will not stand severe frosts so the roots should be clamped in the same way as carrots or beetroot. The exception to this is Golden Ball a small-topped yellow globe, which is one of the finest varieties for autumn sowing.

Turnip top production is often worthwhile. When supplies of greens have been spoiled by bad weather the tops are most useful. For this purpose, make sowings in summer. It may be possible to pull a few bulbs but the roots of the majority will not thicken. Turnips for tops can follow early peas or early potatoes, the seed being sown fairly thickly. Green Top Stone is a suitable variety.

*Varieties include:* for frames and cloches— Early White Frame, Early Milan and Sprinter. Early outdoor sorts—Snowball, Tokyo Cross, an F.1 hybrid; Manchester Market, Jersey Navet and Veitches' Red Globe. For tops— Green Top Stone.

**Vegetable Marrow.** *Cucurbita pepo.* Marrows are not always as highly valued as they might be because they are left to become old and ripe. At that stage they become insipid and then are most useful for making jam. These fruits consist of a large percentage of water, although vitamin A is present, with traces of other good elements.

Marrows like a moist soil although really heavy land is not suitable since it warms up so late. Sandy soil dries out just when the plants need moisture. First sowings can be made in spring on a hot bed where there is a minimum temperature of 15 °C. Seed can be sown either in boxes and pricked out later into pots or sown directly into pots.

Keep the surface soil in the pots from becoming hard otherwise growth will be impeded. Germination will take place within three or four days of sowing. Mice are partial to marrow seeds and they should be prevented from reaching the sown pots. Plenty of ventilation is needed during the daytime and when they are growing well, the plants should be moved to their final quarters in frames.

Make beds for this purpose by digging sites 30 cm. or more deep, and filling them with well rotted manure which should be trodden in, and a covering of soil placed over it. Make the holes at each corner of the frame.

Water as necessary, and keep the lights

101

closed until the plants start growing. In the event of cold nights, straw or hessian can be placed on the frame. When frosts are over the glass can be removed from the frames. A top dressing of dried blood, well watered in will be helpful.

Outdoor crops are fertilised by bees and other insects: under glass it is advisable to hand pollinate. This is best done about midday preferably, when it is sunny and the flowers are dry. The female flower is distinguishable by the embryo fruit seen at the back of the petals. Once fruit has set, regular watering and occasional feeds of liquid manure will be beneficial.

The first outdoor sowings should not be made until cold weather has passed. The resultant plants will produce marrows during summer and autumn.

*Varieties.* Bush Green; compact, bushy growth, dark green fruits with paler stripes. White: same habit as Bush Green, but with creamy-white fruit. Tender and True, a slightly flattened fruit mottled green. In addition there are now a number of F.1 hybrids including Zucchini, early maturing, slender green fruit; Early Gem and Zephyr pale green flecked grey. Custard or Patty Pan, creamy-white, flattish fruits with scalloped edges and a concave base. Trailing: Long Green; Long White; Moore's Cream; smooth, oval-shaped, early.

Marrows can be kept in a dry, frost-proof place for winter use.

The avocadella or avocada marrow from the Argentine is a distinct bush marrow producing grapefruit size fruits usually ribbed like a melon. The skin is jade green, contrasting handsomely with the orange flesh, which is firm and smooth.

Gathered young and cooked whole, they are delicious, but a better way is to use them as a substitute for the avocado pear. For this, cut them in half (as with a grapefruit), remove the seeds and boil for ten minutes; serve with salad cream and other condiments to taste.

Avocadellas can be stored like marrows in a dry, warm place for use as required.

**Vegetable Spaghetti.** This can be grown in exactly the same way as the ordinary vegetable marrow. Seed can be sown in early spring in the greenhouse, the plants being gradually hardened off for planting outdoors when cold weather has passed. The fruits, up to 45 cm. long, are carried on trailing growths. They should be cut when well coloured and for cooking should be boiled up to 30 minutes or can be wrapped in foil and baked in a hot oven until tender. When cut in half the inside comes away just like spaghetti.

**Watercress.** This crop is available over a long period, being particularly useful at times when other salad ingredients are scarce. It has a high mineral content, exceeding that of lettuce and salad onions, while its vitamin C and B.1 content are also high. Its nutritive value depends upon the aromatic oil and mineral ingredients in which it exceeds all other salad plants.

Watercress is divided into two main groups, the green, available in summer, and the brown or winter strains which are most in demand. Watercress can be propagated from seed or cuttings. Seed can be sown throughout the summer. Start with an almost dry seed bed; sprinkle the seed thinly on the surface, then admit a trickle of water to encourage germination. Consolidate the soil to encourage a mat of roots to form. Small quantities of watercress can be raised by sowing seed in a cold frame or in trays or flower pots of moist compost having a high humus content.

Once the plants are growing well, cut the tops off the stems, which will make them branch well and promote a vigorous root system. Plants from seed sown in heat in March should be gradually hardened off before being put in trenches about 15 cm. apart. Keep the sites supplied with moisture and when the plants are growing well, they will benefit from feeds of Liquinure or Maxicrop.

It is easy to propagate watercress from cuttings taken from the sturdy shoots. Do this in May and June for autumn and winter cropping, and in September and October for spring and summer cutting, the brown variety being best at the later time.

9a) Above *Frame Cucumber.*
*For cool greenhouse or cold frame.*

9b) Below *Radish, French Breakfast.*
*Quick growing, mild flavour and tender.*

*10a*) Above  *Salad Alfalfa.*
  *Nutritious sprouts, rich in protein and vitamins.*

*10b*) Below  *Onion, Rijnsburger.*
  *Golden-brown skin, heavy cropping. Good keeper.*

11) *Leek, Catalina.*
   *Mild flavour. Remains in good condition for a long*
   *time.*

Anise
*Pimpinella Anicum*

Angelica (Cultivated form)
*Angelica Archangelica*

Bay
*Laurus Nobilis*

Basil
*Ocimum Basilicum*

Chervil
*Anthriscus Cerefolium*

Fennel
(Root—Florence Fennel)
*Foeniculum Vulgare*

Marjoram
*Origanum Vulgare*

Rosemary
*Rosmarinus Officinalis*

*Common Comfrey*
*Symphytum Officinale*

*Caraway*
*Carum Carvi*

*Chives*
*Allium Schoenoprasum*

*Coriander*
*Coriandrum Sativum*

*Rue*
*Ruta Graveolens*

*Salad Burnet*
*Sanguisorba Minor*

*Sage*
*Salvia Officinalis*

*Common Thyme*
*Thymus Vulgaris*

14) *Tomato, Gardener's Delight.*
   *An outdoor variety with small fruit of sweet flavour.*

*15a)* Above *Melon, Ha-Ogen.*
   *Round fruits. An excellent-flavoured half-hardy*
   *variety.*

*15b)* Below *Lettuce, Webbs Wonderful, A crisp hearty*
   *lettuce.*

*16a)* Above *Broad Bean, Promotion.*
   *High yielding, packed with delicious beans.*

*16b)* Below *Savoy, January Prince.*
   *Rather smaller but just as hardy as January King.*

# CHAPTER SIX

# Herbs,
# Their Cultivation, Values and Uses

**Alecost.** *Tanecetum.* This is a pleasant herb with a scent reminiscent of mint. The roundish leaves are greyish-green the button-like flowers being yellow. Growing 60 to 90 cm. high this subject flourishes in a sunny position where the soil is rich. Finely chopped leaves are useful in salads. Ointment was once made from the leaves and used for soothing burns and bruises.

**Alexanders.** *Smyrinium olustratum.* Sometimes known as Black Lovage, this old wild plant can be found growing on waste places and on cliffs. It also grows well in ordinary garden soil and produces umbels of greenish-yellow scented flowers on 75 to 90 cm. stems. The leaves have a pungent flavour and can be chopped up for including in salads.

**Alkanets.** *Anchusa officinalis.* Not to be confused with borage, this is an ancient plant with long narrow leaves and branching stems of 45 to 60 cm. carrying heads of blue flowers from May to August. At one time a red dye was obtained from the roots and used for staining wood.

**Allspice.** *Calycantha floridus.* This shrub, growing 2 to 2·25 m. high needs to be placed in a sheltered position. The carmine flowers appear in August. The wood of this shrub has the allspice scent which makes this subject worth growing. The commercial allspice comes from one of the pimentoes.

**Angelica.** *Angelica archangelica.* There are several forms of this plant some being wild. The true angelica of confectionary is a native of parts of Russia and Germany.

This plant although a perennial growing 90 cm. to 1·50 m. high usually dies after flowering well. It prefers partial shade and a cool moist but not wet, root run.

Seed can be sown in spring or autumn. The sculptured foliage has a stately appearance, while the thick hollow stems possess an aromatic scent which is retained when they are candied. The young stems are greatly valued when cut up and used in tarts with rhubarb, as well as in jams. A leaf added to salads imparts a pleasing taste, while both foliage and roots have certain medicinal qualities. A tale connected with this plant says that it holds powers against evil spirits.

**Anise.** *Pimpinella.* This annual plant grows about 60 cm. high. An ancient subject thriving in Mediterranean districts, it is referred to several times in the Bible. Sowings can be made in spring the round aromatic seeds being available from late August onwards. They must be properly dried off and can them be used for flavouring cakes, while they have some value for including in various liquers.

**Balm.** *Melissa officinalis.* Not particular as to soil, this plant growing from 90 cm. to 1·3 m. high, has lemon scented leaves and small white flowers in summer. Propagation is easy by division of roots in spring or autumn or seed can be sown in boxes. Thin the plants early and finally move them to their permanent places 60 cm. apart. Although of little commercial value, when dried, the leaves retain the refreshing lemon flavour which makes them useful for poultry stuffings. A leaf or two placed in the tea pot with the tea provides a pleasant drink. A useful bee plant, balm, also known as lemon balm, was once used to soothe the nerves and 'drive away melancholy'.

**Basil.** *Ocymum.* This annual subject a native

of India, is usually treated as a half-hardy. Seed is sown under glass in a temperature of 15°C the plants being moved to the garden in early June. Alternatively, sow outdoors in sandy soil in May. Germination is usually erratic. The irregularly shaped leaves have a pleasant clover-like flavour so useful for including either fresh or dried in soups and stews.

Basil has been cultivated for centuries and is said to 'procure a merrie heart' while at one time it was placed in water used for washing. **Bush Basil.** *O. minimum* grows about 15 cm. high. The so-called Sweet Basil, *O. basilica* is larger but not quite so hardy.

**Bay.** *Laurus nobilis.* This evergreen laurel-like shrub should be grown either in the open ground or in tubs in a sheltered place. Sweet Bay is valued for its leaves both when fresh or dried. Since the flavour is so potent the leaves must be used sparingly. The yellow flowers are often followed by purplish berries. It is best to buy new plants in pots, since transplanting from the open ground is not always successful.

**Bergamot.** *Monarda.* Often known as Bee Balm, this is a perennial plant of which there are many cultivars. Growing up to 90 cm. high, the plants like a cool root run and should never lack moisture in summer. Both leaves and flowers can be included in salads and the leaves may be used fresh or dry to impart an aromatic flavour to the usual Indian or China tea. One common name for bergamot is Oswego Tea. A few leaves chopped fine make a valuable addition to salads and are also useful in pot pourris as well as the scented garden.

**Borage.** *Borago officinalis.* This attractive an-annual growing 45 to 75 cm. high, can be sown in boxes or pots under glass in spring or in the open ground after frosts are over. In addition, sown in well drained soil in September and provided the winter is mild, the plants will flower the following spring. The whole plant is covered with greyish hairs, the flowers being an intense blue. At one time the young leaves were used in salads, the tender growths being boiled and eaten, while leaves and flower tops are used in drinks and the flowers were sometimes candied. An excellent bee plant, it has a cucumber-like fragrance.

**Burnet.** *Sanguisorba minor.* This hardy perennial growing 45 to 50 cm. high, can sometimes be found growing wild. While not of striking appearance, the greenish flowers have red stigmas. Keep the blooms cut to encourage more leaves to develop. The foliage has a cucumber-like flavour with a nutty undertone making it useful for inclusion in salads, soups and cooling drinks. Sow the seed in prepared beds in spring and move the plants to their final positions at the end of the summer.

**Camphor plant.** *Balsamita.* A hardy perennial producing white daisy-like flowers with yellow centres. The leaves emit a refreshing scent when bruised. This subject should not be confused with Cinnamonum camphora, the plant from which commercial oil is obtained.

**Caper Spurge.** *Euphorbia lathyrus.* An ancient plant of biennial habit. This is another subject often found growing wild. The upright stems are clothed with stiff narrow leaves, the small greenish flowers being followed by fruits sometimes used as a substitute for capers. This plant is sometimes recommended to keep away moles. It is the liquid secreted in the roots that is effective for this purpose and therefore the plants are not really mole deterrents until their second season.

**Caraway.** *Carum carvi.* A biennial plant about 75 cm. high. Seed is sown in well drained soil in spring, the umbels of flowers appearing the following year, the seeds ripening in summer. It is easy to lose seed if the heads remain too long. The stems should be cut as the seeds ripen. Hang them to dry over paper so that the seeds can be caught as they become ripe and fall. Caraway seeds are often used in cakes or for sprinkling on bread, while they have their uses for flavouring soups and cheese dishes.

**Chamomile.** *Anthemis nobilis.* Chamomiles are known for their value for making dwarf lawns. A. nobilis is used for this purpose although it is the 'Teague' form which is the most valuable, since it does not flower and is propagated by division. The more chamomile is trodden on, the more it spreads, and emits its aromatic scent.

Chamomile flowers are often used for making a 'tea'. For this, up to 1 oz. of fresh flowers are covered by a pint of boiling water, the strained liquid being a harmless sedative and a cure for indigestion troubles. The flowers can be used in the preparation of shampoos.

**Chervil.** *Anthriscus.* An annual growing 30 to 45 cm. of which seed should be sown in small amounts frequently. A fairly rich soil that does not dry out should be selected, sowing being done throughout spring. Allow 15 to 18 cm. between the plants. Chervil is included in mixed herbs for improving the taste of soups and salads.

**Chenopodium.** See Good King Henry.

**Chicory.** *Cichorium.* Sometimes known as Succory, this is a hardy perennial, growing 90 cm. to 1·50 m. high. Closely related to the endives this pleasing plant produces pretty light blue flowers in summer. Seed is sown throughout the spring. For forcing lift the roots of Witloof chicory in November and plant closely in boxes of sandy soil. These should be placed under the greenhouse staging or other dark place where a temperature of 13 to 16°C can be provided. Apply water to keep the soil just moist. The blanched heads are used when they are 10 to 13 cm. high. In the open ground, the leaves can be blanched by placing inverted pots over the plants covering the drainage holes. The Magdeburg chicory is the form grown for its dried roots which are ground and used in coffee blending.

**Chives.** *Allium.* This is a perennial onion which if chopped finely is excellent for use in salads and omelettes. Easy to grow, it can be used as an edging plant. It produces mauve-pink flowers which are useful for decorating the salad dish. It is best to prevent flowers from developing but if they do, never let them seed. Cut the plants frequently for this encourages a supply of young shoots. It is best to cut some shoots from each plant and not to denude individual specimens. Excellent for growing in pots and window boxes, the plants divide easily in spring or autumn while seed is sometimes available.

**Clary.** *Salvia sclarea.* In this large family of plants there are a number of species that have long been recognised for their medicinal value and for flavouring as well as being decorative garden plants. One of the common names of the clary sage is Clear Eye since it was once prescribed as a herb to include in the making of eye ointment. The tips of the young shoots as well as the flowers have been used in salads and in various cooking recipes. In addition, the leaves of these decorative plants will impart flavour to soups and stews in much the same way as the more widely used sage.

A biennial, *Salvia sclarea* can be raised from seed sown in late spring. The wrinkled leaves can be gathered during the summer of the following year. The plant grows about 60 cm. high. The actual flowers are lavender and white but it is the striking mauve-pink bracts that make the plant so showy.

In seed catalogues the annual *Salvia horminum* is often referred to as Clary. This is a different plant but quite worth growing for its gaily coloured bracts, frequently referred to as 'flowers'.

**Comfrey.** *Symphytum officinale.* This has the common name of Knit Bone. It flourishes in shady parts of the garden and needs to be kept under control for the smallest pieces of root will grow. This was once a popular fodder crop, producing several cuttings annually.

At one time leaves, which when crushed have a pleasant smell, were used as an application to sprains, bruises and swellings in the form

*Chives*

of a poultice. There is reason to believe that the leaves and roots contain properties helpful in the case of inflammatory troubles. Comfrey tea is an old cure for colds and coughs. Comfrey pills and ointments are now available. Investigations into the value of this plant for other healing purposes are continuing.

Propagation is by root cuttings taken in autumn or clumps of fleshy roots can be divided in spring or summer. The clear blue flowers appear on 1·25 to 1·50 m. stems in late spring.

**Coriander.** *Coriander sativum.* An annual herb growing up to 60 cm. high, the plants produce the round seed frequently used to flavour confectionery and curries. Sow the seeds thinly in a sunny situation. The pale mauve flowers appear in summer and once the seed begins to ripen, the stems should be cut and dried. A frame or other warm place is ideal for the purpose. Do not be disturbed about the unpleasant aroma which comes from the drying stems and leaves. This is temporary. The ripened seed has a pleasant perfume.

**Corn Salad.** *Valarianella olitoria.* Sometimes referred to as Lamb's Lettuce there are now several good improved cultivated forms. Easily grown, it forms a useful substitute for lettuce during the winter for it is hardy. In appearance it is not unlike the Forget-me-Not without the blue flowers, and it makes an excellent cloche crop. It is eaten either raw or cooked. Sowings can be made at intervals during summer and early autumn which will provide supplies from autumn to spring.

Sow thinly in drills 30 cm. apart and since germination is sometimes erratic, sowing is best done in showery weather. The young plants should be thinned so they stand about 15 cm. apart. When harvesting, the leaves should be taken off individually. The broad leaves of large-leaved English Corn Salad is vigorous growing, usually producing plenty of leaves. The Italian strain is less hardy and most suitable for warmer districts. There is a form having greyish-green leaves but it is not so popular.

**Costmary.** See Alecost.

**Cowslip.** *Primula veris.* This well known plant was once found growing in quantity in meadows in various parts of Britain. It has several common names, one being Paigles, another Key flower, the latter because the pendant flowers resemble a bunch of yellow keys. Seed can be sown in spring as soon as new crop is available. If not sown soon after it is ripe the seed is often slow to germinate. This plant was once used for a number of medicinal purposes. One was to make Cowslip syrup used to calm anyone suffering from nervous excitement.

**Cumin.** A very ancient plant referred to several times in the Bible where the spelling Cummin is used. An annual, it grows wild in Egypt and other eastern countries. In mild districts, cumin can be grown outdoors in a sunny, well drained position, sowing the seed late spring. Alternatively, sow under glass a little earlier. The aromatic seeds can be harvested in summer. They are used for flavouring bread and cheese and in Eastern countries, they are added to curry. The leaves are fennel-like, the flowers a dull magenta colour.

**Dandelion.** *Taraxacum officinale.* Usually considered to be a nuisance in any garden, this plant is quite ornamental with its ragged leaves,

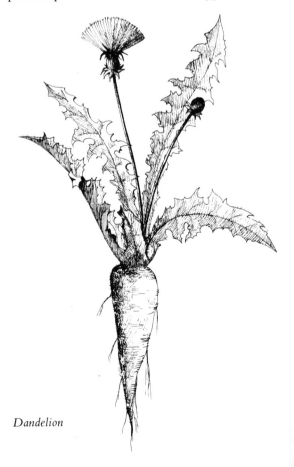

*Dandelion*

brilliant yellow flowers and fairy-like seed heads. A medieval title for the plant was Priest's Crown, the name dandelion being a derivative of Lion's Tooth because of the dentate leaves.

The qualities of the plant exceed its appearance. In salads, the leaves which contain iron and other vitamins, impart a sharp taste. If the leaves are blanched by covering the plants with inverted flower pots they become a useful substitute for lettuce. Wine can be made from the flowers and after being roasted and ground, the roots can be used for making 'coffee'. The whole plant is of value for its blood cleansing properties.

**Dill.** *Anethum.* Another annual for sowing in spring. It will grow in ordinary soil and the plants should be spaced 20 to 23 cm. apart. The young succulent leaves are useful in salads and they can also be used in soups and sauces. The seeds or fruits are also employed in the making of Dill water.

**Elecampane.** *Inula.* This is a showy hardy perennial plant often grown in the flower border and reaching a height of 2 to 2·5 m. It likes sun and a well drained soil which should not dry out in summer. The stems are clothed with large leaves and clusters of shaggy yellow flowers in summer. Propagation is by division of plants in spring or autumn, or seed sown under glass in spring. At one time the roots of elecampane were widely used in the making of candies as a remedy for coughs.

**Fennel.** *Foenoculum vulgare.* Hardy perennials, the plants grow 1·25 to 2 m. high and have finely cut foliage and heads or umbels of yellow flowers. These are often followed by aromatic seeds.

Almost any well drained soil suits fennel although a sheltered position is liked. Plants are raised from seed sown in spring and the foliage can be cut in early autumn, while individual leaves can be gathered and used during summer. The leaves have a pleasantly acid taste which is why they are used in fish and other dishes, while they have been included in the preparation of gripe water. It was once recommended to be eaten by people considered to be overweight.

**Florence fennel** is *F. dulce finocchio* grown for its swollen 'bulb' which has a delicate flavour when braised or used raw in salads. It is much liked in Italy and other European countries.

**Good King Henry.** *Chenopodium bonus henricus.* An ancient plant of hardy constitution. While dormant this plant carries a number of crowns similar to those of rhubarb. In early spring they open to produce small green leaves, followed by light green fleshy shoots which bear at their growing points, clusters of green leaves. These should be gathered and eaten in the same way as asparagus which they resemble in flavour and for which they can be used as a substitute.

When young, these shoots are useful for including raw in salads. The more mature leaves should be cooked and eaten as spinach. Six or twelve shoots can be tied in bundles and gently cooked with just enough water to cover. The thick fleshy roots can be cooked and served with hot melted butter.

Good King Henry is sometimes known as Mercury or All Good. Seed can be sown in the spring, the plants being finally spaced about 30 cm. apart. Unlike asparagus, the plants can be cut the first year after planting. This subject is valued because it is rich in iron and other health giving properties.

**Horehound.** *Marrubium.* A perennial growing

*Good King Henry*

115

60 cm. high this plant has dead-nettle-like leaves and small white flowers. It grows in dryish positions but has no ornamental value apart from its greyish leaves. It has been used in the preparation of cough cures and for flavouring drinks. The so-called black Horehound has mauve-pink flowers.

**Hound's Tongue.** *Cynoglossum officinalis.* This is a biennial of which the foliage is greyish-green and the small flowers, crimson. Plants can often be found growing wild. It is the roots which were once used in the making of pills for curing coughs and colds.

**Hyssop.** *Hyssopus officinalis.* An old fashioned shrubby perennial plant, this subject will make a nice low hedge 60 to 75 cm. high. A native of southern Europe, hyssop likes light soil and plenty of sunshine. It can be clipped annually to retain shapeliness but such action will mean some loss of the two-lipped gentian-blue flowers. Forms having pink or purplish flowers are sometimes available and seedlings from these, often exhibit intermediate colourings.

Propagation is by seed sown under glass in early spring or in the open ground in summer, while cuttings of strong shoots can also be secured in summer. Hyssop is not much used as a herb since the flavour is rather strong. Very few leaves finely chopped are sufficient to include with mixed herbs or in the salad bowl. Hyssop tea made from the dried flowers and used with honey is of value for chest troubles, while an infusion of the green tops is of use in relieving coughs and catarrh.

**Lovage.** *Legisticum officinale.* This hardy perennial has handsome polished foliage, the scent of the whole plant being reminiscent of celery and parsnips with an extra sweetness. A native of Mediterranean areas it has been grown in Europe for centuries, probably being introduced by the Romans. The plants grow best in semi-shade or sun, in rich moist soil, reaching a height of 1·25 m. the umbels of yellowish flowers opening in summer. Propagation is by seed sown in spring or division in spring and autumn. Lovage was once greatly favoured for use in the form of a tissane in cases of fever and colic. It can be used as a substitute for celery and is normally available fresh or dry.

**Mace.** *Achillea decolorans.* The true mace is myristisa a tropical fruit, but the leaves of this achillea are often used as a substitute 'mace' for flavouring soups and stews. A hardy plant, growing 45 cm. high with cut-edged leaves and creamy daisy-like flowers, it flourishes in good soil in unexposed positions. The plants divide easily in spring or autumn.

**Marjoram** *origanum.* This small genus of plants is valued for its colour, scent and in the case of some varieties, their culinary flavourings. It was once used as a remedy for eye troubles associated with poor health. O. marjarama the Knotted Marjoram, has small greyish aromatic leaves. A hardy perennial, it is often raised from seed sown under glass in early spring and planted outdoors in summer.

**O. vulgare** is the wild English species often known as the Pot Marjoram. Growing 45 to 50 cm. high, it has various forms. O. aureum is the golden marjoram with soft yellow, scented leaves and pink flowers.

**Mercury.** See Good King Henry.

**Mint.** *Mentha.* M. *spicata* or *viridis* is the best known species. Often referred to as spearmint it is also known as mackerel mint, pea or potato mint, and green lamb mint. The leaves are sometimes infused and are frequently used for the troubles of infants. This species, growing 1·25 m. high, is distinguished by its pointed glossy, dark green leaves. Of invasive habit, it should be divided frequently or propagated from cuttings.

*Mentha rotundifolia* often known as the Apple or Royal mint, is fairly strong growing with large leaves, being excellent for mint sauce and for flavouring jellies. Less susceptible to 'rust' than other species it should be grown where that trouble has been prevalent. It is disliked by some people because of its rather hairy or woolly leaves.

*Mentha peperita* is seldom grown. It has several common names including Brandy Mint and Balm mint. It is from the distillation of the purple flower heads of this species that oil of peppermint is obtained.

A number of menthas not suitable for eating, have for centuries been cherished for their aroma in sachets and for keeping moths out of stored linen. Particularly good is M. *citrata* Eau de Cologne, which when rubbed, can be mistaken for the well known perfume. Other mints include one with a ginger scent, and another with variegated foliage which has a penetrating scent not unlike pineapple, which was much used by Victorian ladies in their posies of lavender and rosemary. Old herbals recommend mint infusions for stomach troubles and head colds.

Mint is of simple propagation easy to divide. Established plants are easy to split, quite small pieces of root producing sturdy plants in a short time. Succulent growths can be obtained during winter for the plants force readily.

**Pennyroyal.** *Mentha pulegium.* A neat growing plant particularly suitable where space is limited. A dwarf carpeting subject with pink flowers, it can be grown in the rock garden or used as an edging. There is also a less common upright form which is the best for harvesting and drying. These plants like a cool, moist soil. The foliage is powerfully flavoured so that it should be used with discretion for culinary purposes. Plants of pennyroyal are easily increased by division in spring or autumn.

**Purslane.** *Portulaca.* This is a herb which is much valued in Eastern countries, although it has also been grown in Europe for centuries. An annual with succulent foliage, it thrives in light soil, and likes the sun. The young leaves can be cooked or used raw in salads and sandwiches, while they impart a special flavour to soups. Sow the seeds in spring in small batches to ensure succession. Allow 15 cm. between plants with the rows 23 cm. apart. These plants transplant well but should never want for moisture.

**Rampion.** *Campanula rapunculus.* A well known pot herb, this is a true bellflower a member of the campanula family. A biennial, it forms a tap root and in the first year produces a rosette of leaves. The second season the bluebell-like flowers appear on 60 to 90 cm. stems in summer. The tiny seed needs careful sowing in spring. Choose a light well drained site, the addition of peat or leaf mould being helpful in retaining moisture and encouraging the roots to develop to a good size. Some gardeners earth up the plants to provide winter protection. The roots can be dug in late autumn onwards and stored in dryish sand for use as required.

The flowers are quite ornamental although if not required they should be cut before seed sets, otherwise self-sown seedlings become a nuisance.

**Rosemary.** *Rosmarinus officinalis.* This is one of the best known herbs around which there are many legends. An excellent bee plant, it is the shrub of remembrance and friendship, the phrase 'rosemary for remembrance' being very well known. It is eulogised in old books, one stating that 'it comforteth the heart and maketh merry and lively'.

It has a powerful flavour and one or two leaves are sufficient to add to soup and stews. Rosemary has a number of uses including the making of a hair wash and flavouring sugar, while dried leaves make a useful addition to pot pourri. The narrow dark green leaves are silvery beneath, the pretty blue flowers appearing in spring. The type grows about 90 cm. high and with regular clipping after flowering will remain in good condition for many years. Sun and good drainage suits these plants. There is a very rare variegated form and another known as Miss Jessops' Upright. Of stiff erect habit it is useful for hedges since it grows 1·25 to 1·50 m. high.

**Rue.** *Ruta graveolans.* A well known shrubby

*Rampion*

117

plant concerning which there are legends attached to its uses. One is that it is a symbol of 'repentance and regret'. It was once carried by judges at the opening of Assizes, in the belief that it kept off gaol fever. The plant has a penetrating scent appreciated by some people, disliked by others. A perennial growing 60 to 90 cm. high, in severe winters the foliage may be damaged but usually the leaves are attractive during the dark days. This applies especially to the forms having bluish-green leaves.

Seed can be sown in spring or cuttings of young shoots made in summer. Rue succeeds in a sunny site and in a medium loam. Chopped leaves are useful in salads while rue tea is said to have stimulating qualities.

**Sage.** *Salvia officinalis.* There are three main types of sage, those with grey-green leaves, green leaves or reddish foliage. Under normal cultivation they grow 60 to 75 cm. high. The common sage, a native of Europe, has been grown in Britain since 1597. The greyish leaves are about 38 mm. long, the purple bell-shaped flowers opening in summer. The plants need a well drained soil.

Propagation is by seed or division. It is simple to pull off rooted pieces for growing separately. If the soil is drawn toward the plants, the lower parts of the stems will form roots and they can be severed from the parent plant and grown individually.

While the broad leafed species is best for drying, the narrow leafed and variegated forms are also useful. There are some forms producing pink and white flowers. The aim should be to concentrate on non-flowering types which are best where leaves for drying, flavouring and stuffing are required.

**Savory.** *Satureja.* Well known by name but little grown, there are two forms, winter and summer. The former an annual, is raised from seed sown in spring in a sunny position in drills 30 cm. apart. Choose a light rich soil, and thin the seedlings so there is 15 cm. between them. Winter Savory is a perennial of which the roots are divided in spring, or cuttings of new shoots can be taken in spring. This one does best on a rather poor soil. Fresh sprays of savory can be used for garnishing and as a substitute for mint when boiling potatoes or beans. The leaves can also be dried and used for stuffing.

**Smallage.** *Apium graveolens* var. This is the wild celery once quite widely used medicinally as a remedy for rheumatism and other joint disorders. Seed is rarely if ever offered in seedsmens catalogues but plants can sometimes be found growing in rough areas along the seashore.

**Sorrel.** *Rumex acetosa.* This is plentiful in our fields and countryside, and can be used for salads. *R. scutatus* is the French Sorrel which is best, being much less acid and not running to seed so quickly. The plants are grown for their leaves which add a piquant flavour to summer salads. They can also be mixed with spinach and used in soups. Seed should be sown in spring in rows 45 cm. apart, the plants being thinned to 30 cm. Roots can be divided in spring since this is a perennial plant. The flower stems must be nipped out as they appear. A few plants potted and brought into the greenhouse in spring will provide early pickings. It is best to remove the leaves singly from the plants alternatively, they can be treated as annuals and the whole plant cut as soon as the leaves are of good size.

**Sweet Cicely.** *Myrrhis odorata.* This is a decorative plant with large fern-like leaves. A hardy subject with a thickish tap root, it can sometimes be found growing wild in semi-shady dampish positions. It normally grows about 75 to 90 cm. high, but older plants grow taller. The umbels of white flowers are freely produced in early summer.

It is best to cut the flowers before they open if the leaves are required for flavouring. Both roots and leaves can be used in salads to which they impart a faint aniseed flavour. Chopped leaves are sometimes added to sugared strawberries, while they have some value in reducing the acidity in sour or tart fruit, lessening the quantity of sugar required.

Propagation is by seed sown in spring, although it is also possible to carefully divide roots.

**Tansy.** *Tanacetum.* Flourishing under almost any condition and sometimes seen growing by the roadside, this perennial plant has feathery foliage brilliant yellow button-like flowers in summer and a refreshing lemon scent. Growing 1 to 1·5 m. high, it was once widely grown in cottage gardens for its medicinal and flavouring qualities. It is said to be one of the ingredients of the bitter herbs eaten by Jews at the celebration of the Passover. Tansy tea is still sometimes used as a cure for feverish colds and as a spring tonic.

**Thyme.** *Thymus vulgaris.* This family of plants varies in size from the creeping form, *T. serpyllum,* to those making bushes of up to 60 cm. high. All like sun and to be sheltered from cutting winds, while well drained soil containing humus matter leads to the required leafy growth. Harvesting must be carried out before the flowers appear.

The common thyme is essential in any concoction of mixed herbs and in the past it has had the reputation of 'promoting courage and vitality'. The flowers are attractive to bees and it is sometimes possible to obtain so-called Thyme Honey.

Used fresh or dry its flavour improves the taste of many culinary dishes and is invaluable in stuffings, although it needs to be used wisely. Oil of thyme is used for several medicinal purposes.

*T. citriodora.* The lemon Thyme has a refreshing, less pungent flavour, often used in stuffings and with fish. T. herba borona has scent reminiscent of caraway. Besides its culinary uses, it is excellent for the rock garden.

**Valerian.** *Valeriana officinalis.* This is the true valerian sometimes known as All Heal, and not Kentranthus ruber, the plant commonly seen growing on walls, railway banks and in cottage gardens. The true valerian has greyish foliage and very pale pink flowers. Hardy perennials, the plants grow 90 to 105 cm. high and like a moist, fairly rich soil to encourage the rhizomatous roots to swell. These roots contain oil and alkaloids used in medicine chiefly on account of the sedative qualities, but also for nervous disorders.

**Wormwood.** *Artemesia absinthium.* Also known as Old Woman and Mugwort, this shrubby plant has decorative gracefully cut, greyish foliage which provides a pleasing effect against the background of bigger darker leaved subjects. Growing about 45 cm. high, it has yellow flowers in summer.

# CHAPTER SEVEN

# *Growing Tomatoes*

Records show that the tomato, *Lycopersicum esculentum*, has been known and grown for many centuries. Natives of South America these plants came to Europe in the Seventeenth century when they were cultivated as ornamental subjects under the name of Love Apples.

There are many varieties of wild tomatoes of which the fruit differs considerably in shape, size and colour. They vary in height, some if not checked growing many feet, others being dwarf and bushy.

The fruit contains vitamin C, although the juice of the fruit is less valuable than that of blackcurrants, strawberries or oranges. Vitamin B1 is also present, but it is their vitamin A content that makes tomatoes so valuable.

Whether being grown outdoors or under glass, the plants are raised in a similar way. Since the seeds are large and can be handled individually they should be spaced 12 mm. apart in boxes or pans of a clean seed sowing compost. Cover the seeds well, then place glass and paper over the boxes to exclude light.

For quickest results, keep the receptacles in a temperature of 18 to 20°C. After a few days, growth will be seen and the covering can be removed. Once the seed leaves open, each seedling can be transferred separately into small pots or soil blocks.

When they have settled in the pots, the temperature can be reduced by 2 or 3 degrees with free ventilation. Only first class seedlings should be potted up. Plants with fern-like leaves are known as rogues or 'jacks' and should be discarded.

A good way of producing really strong plants is to maintain a fairly even temperature. When the heat varies, irregular growth is produced. Sturdy, short jointed plants of a deep green colour are likely to be the most fruitful. Avoid long jointed, hard, wiry stemmed plants.

It is the practice of commercial growers to sow from mid-winter onwards where fruit is required from late spring onwards. The majority of amateur gardeners sow in succession to obtain a longer fruiting period.

It is never wise to put tomatoes outdoors until danger of cold weather has passed. Allow 38 to 45 cm. between the plants and if a double row is being used, 45 cm. should be between them. Bush types need wide spacing, say 60 cm. between the plants and 75 cm. between rows. Staking should be done immediately after planting, the ties being made as growth proceeds.

Disturb the roots as little as possible. Pot grown plants are easy to knock out. Those raised in boxes can be carefully removed. For these, first cut the roots down to the bottom of the box in the shape of a cube, then lift each one with plenty of soil. Place them firmly in position so there is 12 mm. of soil above the roots.

Standard varieties are usually grown on a single stem, all side shoots being removed while they are small. They can also be grown on double or treble stems depending on their strength. It is rarely worthwhile allowing outdoor plants to carry more than four trusses of fruit for there is insufficient time for more fruit to ripen. Pinch out growing points in late summer, even if they have only formed three trusses. When buying plants choose a named

*Tomato, Seville. Heavy cropping and reliable.*

variety from a known source.

Tomatoes thrive in the warm greenhouse where there is an absence of draughts, good ventilation and a minimum night temperature of around 12°C. For preference, use a greenhouse glazed to ground level if the plants are to be grown in the 'floor' or border. Otherwise, the beds will have to be raised or made up on the staging. Alternatively, grow the pants in large pots or deep boxes.

Whether outdoors or indoors, tomatoes like fairly rich root conditions. Strawy horse manure is ideal but difficult to obtain. Among good substitutes used by growers are moist wheat straw, well dusted with hoof and horn manure, ripe compost, well decayed seaweed or spent hops. Peat or leaf mould help to increase the humus content and provide bulk which encourages plenty of roots to develop. Add lime as necessary.

At planting time, make sure the sub-soil is moist. Beds on the staging can be made up with the same soil mixture. Place asbestos or a similar covering over the slats, followed by drainage material. Boards 23 to 25 cm. wide, should be fixed to the front of the staging, to get the proper root depth when the compost is added. This need only be 13 cm. deep at first. Add more compost as growth proceeds, so the soil level comes to within 25 mm. of the top of the board.

Liquid manure should be given at ten day intervals once the first trusses of fruits have set. For plants in pots or boxes, a simple soil mixture on the basis of the John Innes potting compost No. 2, can be used.

Plants must be thoroughly hardened off before being planted out. Make sure they are well watered some time before they are knocked out of their pots. Set the plants 45 cm. apart allowing 60 cm. between rows. In larger plantings, leave an alleyway of 90 cm. to

121

*Tomato, Royal Ace. Medium-sized good coloured fruit. Disease resistant.*

1·20 m. after every four rows to make it easier for cleaning the soil, removing side shoots and fruit gathering.

Plant with a trowel and press the soil firmly around the roots so the root ball and garden soil are in close contact. Do not water the plants unless the surrounding soil is on the dry side. If the weather turns cold as soon as the tomatoes have been planted, place cloches, large pots or newspapers over them at night but remove them the next morning.

The plants selected for growing on should be short jointed, stocky, of good colour and about 20 to 30 cm. high. It is best to place supports in position before planting. This ensures that no damage is done to the roots, but the plants can be supported and kept upright at once.

If they fall about, the stems may become 'kinked'. As the plants grow, keep them tied to supports with soft string or wide raffia. Leave room in the tie for the stems to expand. Where really large, heavy trusses of fruit

*Tying Tomatoes*

develop, these should be looped to the main stem to prevent breakage of the truss stem. Keep side shoots removed while small.

Hot days followed by warm humid nights are ideal for the full natural setting of the fruit. In hot, dry weather light overhead sprayings of water can be given in the evening but do

122

*Tomato, Sigmabush. An outstanding bush variety.*

this with care to avoid the crippling blight disease.

Tomatoes can be grown successfully in frames of various kinds, and barn cloches are also suitable. Place these structures in a fairly open, yet sheltered position, preferably running north and south. This will encourage good growth.

Planting is usually done in early spring. A bed of fairly rich soil should be made up, well moistened peat being useful for encouraging a good root system. Good supports will be needed. Keep the frame covered until June giving plenty of ventilation whenever the weather is favourable. Plants under tall frames can be supported by wire or string and canes.

Tomatoes do well under cloches in a sunny site and where there is shelter from winds. With the exception of those planted in light soil, take out a trench 18 cm. deep and 30 cm. wide at the top, tapering to the bottom. Prepare early, applying good organic fertiliser and plenty of peat at the base to provide proper growing conditions.

## Planting outdoors

Tomatoes are most accommodating plants but when they are to be grown outdoors a really good start under the right conditions is essential to ensure complete success.

Since they are frost tender, weather conditions and the state of the soil must be such that growth continues unchecked once the plants have been placed in the open ground. It is not wise to do this until frosts have passed.

Many gardeners now use hormone setting sprays when atmospheric conditions are unsuitable for natural fertilisation, or where growth is rank and flowers fail to set fruit. With good culture these aids should not be necessary, but it is important to get the bottom truss of fruit to set for this encourages even, healthy growth and improves both the quality and setting tendency of later trusses.

Intermittent drying out and heavy watering leads to irregular growth as well as cracked fruit. A surface mulching of peat, leaf mould, or similar material will help to maintain a cool root run which is beneficial to the plants, and

123

prevents the surface soil from drying out.

On deep well prepared land, artificial watering is seldom needed. If it can be avoided so much the better, for continued watering brings the roots near the surface, where they suffer from dryness much more than when they are deep in the soil.

If the soil has been well prepared and enriched, it should be unnecessary to give extra feeding. Should growth become extra luxuriant and rank, a dressing of seaweed manure scattered round the plants and watered in, will help to steady development.

Outdoors, it should easily be possible to bring three trusses of fruit to maturity. If the position is warm and sheltered and the weather good, a fourth truss can sometimes be allowed. There is not point in allowing plants to waste their strength on growth and flowers from which it is impossible to secure fruit. When the chosen number of trusses has been selected, the plants should be stopped at one leaf beyond the top truss and from that time, one or two side shoots can be allowed to develop.

This will keep the sap flowing and discourage fruit splitting which sometimes occurs once the plants have been stopped. The excess of sap then goes into the fruit, which cannot expand fast enough, causing the skin to crack, particularly if heavy rains follow a period of dry weather. Discoloured and old leaves can be removed, which will improve air circulation as well as help to lessen the possibility or spread of blight.

Gather the fruit as soon as it is well coloured. In some districts birds will peck the fruit once it is tinted. Often they are only seeking moisture, so it is helpful to place shallow containers of water near the plants. This also works among other crops, both vegetables and flowers, which birds sometimes attack, particularly during spells of hot, dry weather.

If in autumn some fruit is still unripe, the complete trusses should be cut off and hung up in the warm greenhouse or living room. Alternatively, fruits can be gathered individually and wrapped in paper and placed in a drawer or box, where warmth and darkness will bring out the colour. Kept in this way, ripening fruit will be available over a period of weeks.

*Pinching out Tomatoes*

**Autumn and winter fruiting**
By careful planning, ripe fruit will be available from the greenhouse well after the summer, a time when fresh fruit is appreciated. For late fruiting, seed should be sown towards the end of spring using boxes of good compost which have a layer of peat placed at the bottom. For a winter crop sow in summer. Space the seed at least 25 mm. apart and cover the boxes with paper to prevent them drying out. Remove the covering once germination occurs. This spacing results in the minimum root disturbance at pricking off time.

It also allows seedlings to be moved straight from the seed boxes to small 60 size pots, larger sizes being given as growth develops. By the time 20 to 23 cm. pots are reached, the plants should be sturdy and in full growth. Keep them under cool conditions for a week or two. Then stand outdoors in a sheltered place for a couple of months.

For the final potting, provide a good layer of drainage crocks and use a soil mixture such as four parts turfy loam, one part of strawy horse manure, and a good sprinkling of hoof and horn meal, or wood ash. While outside, feed the plants with liquid manure. This encourages short, stocky growth and strong fruit trusses. Fish meal can be lightly worked into the surface soil and in the pots and watered in. Take the plants into the greenhouse towards the end of summer. Air and light are essential, with a night temperature of 10°C. The ripening process will be slow, but the fruit colours up evenly.

## Ring Culture

The ring culture of tomatoes is now widely practiced. It is a method which provides controlled conditions of nourishment and water supply. It was first practiced at the Tilgate Horticultural Research Station in Sussex.

Because of indifferent crops then being produced, it was decided to grow greenhouse tomatoes in some large bottomless earthen-

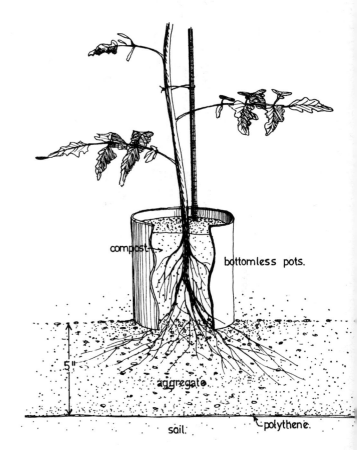

*Tomato ring culture*

*Repotting Tomatoes*

125

ware rings or containers. These rings were filled with compost and planted in the usual way. By chance some of the rings had been placed on a tiled floor such as found in old conservatories and growing rooms, and some or part of the floor which had been covered with ashes from a coal fired boiler.

It was found that the plants standing over the ash grew much more freely and cropped much more heavily. Since all plants were grown in the same compost and had the same attention no answer could be at first found for their greatly differing results.

When the rings were moved it was discovered that it was the plants which had grown over the ash base that had fruited so heavily. They had made a strong secondary root system in the ash layer which had remained damp allowing the roots to spread out widely. The plants standing over the tiles had their roots restricted to the rings.

Rings of widely varied materials have been used, and apart from weathered ashes, many other materials have been employed on which to stand the rings. These layers are known as aggregates, and among those now used are small grade clinkers, sand, crushed ballast and peat. Gravel can be used but is not so moisture retentive as the other materials. The same applies to stone chippings and very coarse clinkers. The depth of the aggregate is not important except that it should not be less than 10 cm. although there does not seem any advantage in going beyond 15 cm.

Although not essential, where there has previously been trouble from disease or eelworm, an effective way of isolating the aggregate layer from the greenhouse soil is to first provide a layer of polythene, or even concrete for a more permanent separation. In either case some provision must be made for the escape of surplus water, although the aggregate must be kept constantly moist so that the lower zone of roots never dries out. Any possibility of waterlogging resulting in unhealthy root action must be avoided.

Where there is sufficient height, tomatoes can be grown in rings on greenhouse benches, for provided shade is given, the plants can be trained to the roof. There is no problem in growing tomatoes in rings in the open ground, although it is best to select a south facing site. If the aggregate layer is raised a little above the surrounding soil it prevents compost being washed into or rain beaten over, the aggregate. Alternatively boards can be placed round the aggregate to keep it intact.

The John Innes Compost No. 3 was used in the initial trials and properly made, it is not so liable to dry out as 'ordinary' composts which are often too light, depending on the type of loam used. This perhaps is not so important once the secondary roots in the aggregate are working well. When they are not and the feeding roots in the rings dry out, the foliage may wilt and some of the flowers fall before they set.

Here perhaps is the place to mention the size of the rings. It is now possible to buy a number of types of bituminised cardboard and similar material. A good size is 20 cm. deep with a top diameter of 23 cm. Having made a 5 to 8 cm. layer of compost firm on the bottom of the ring (placed on the aggregate) the tomato plant should be taken from its pot and placed firmly in the ring pressing the soil closely around the ball of roots without damaging them. Bring the soil to within 4 cms. of the top of the ring this space being left for watering and then for feeding. Then give a good watering so the roots settle in their new compost.

After about ten days, apply water close to the plant stem, (this is ball watering) and make the aggregate wet and keep it so. After a month or so roots will be penetrating the aggregate and ball watering should cease, all moisture then being drawn through the secondary root system. By this time the nutrients in the rings will be almost exhausted and feeding into the rings at seven day intervals should be commenced.

Do not water into the rings after feeding until it is evident that the compost is becoming dry. Lack of free moisture in the container causes the foliage to droop a little and lose its fresh lively colour.

It is always best to feed in solution, since with the comparatively little watering into the rings there is less opportunity for the solid feed to be carried to the fibrous roots.

The fertiliser first used on tomatoes grown in rings was known as 667 from the analysis of

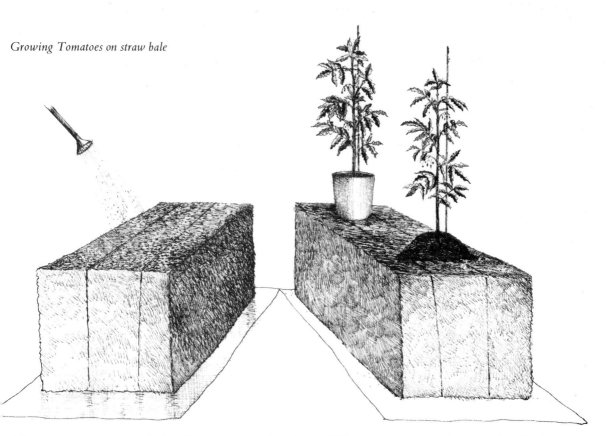

6% each of nitrogen and phosphoric acid, and 7% potash which provides the necessary magnesium for good colour. Once the first truss has set, liquid organic fertiliser should be given at seven day intervals. It is now possible to obtain a number of really good non-forcing organic fertilisers with a similar analysis.

One must bear in mind that plants in rings do require more feeding than those in the border. Otherwise they become half-starved, growth is indifferent, and the quality and quantity of the fruit poor.

The removal of side shoots and general attention needed by tomatoes in rings is the same as that required by plants grown under the usual method.

## Straw Bale Culture

The technique of growing tomatoes on straw bales has grown out of work done some years ago at the Lee Valley Horticultural Experimental Station in Hertfordshire.

Among basic advantages of straw-bale cultivation is isolation from soil-borne troubles of which tomato mosaic virus may be among the most destructive. Root debris from a previous crop is also known as a source of disease infection which cannot always be entirely eliminated by the general methods of soil sterilisation.

Start with a bale of clean straw. Place this broadside downwards in the soil border of the greenhouse, or to provide extra head room for plants in a low house, the bale can be sunk by removing 30 to 60 cm. of soil. If the bales are laid flat on sheets of thin gauge polythene extending 15 cm. beyond the sides of the bales, it helps to prevent infection of the straw from the soil. Soak the bale with frequent drenchings of water over a period of two or three days. Pierce the straw with a sharp rod of some kind to aid water penetration. If hot water can be applied, this softens the straw more quickly.

Liquid fertiliser must be applied evenly and are best used in accordance with the directions supplied with them. A sprinkling of nitro-chalk before application of the liquid will hasten the break down of the straw.

A greenhouse temperature of around 10°C is needed to induce fermentation. After a couple of days the straw will begin to heat, rising to 38 to 49°C. Wait a few days before bringing the plants into the greenhouse or they will become scorched.

The next step is to make a 'trough' 15 cm. deep 30 cm. wide, down the centre of the bales, or separate stations 15 cm. deep and 30 to 38 cm. apart each way are suitable. Fill them with good compost and allow this to warm through for a couple of days before setting out the plants. The heat produced in the bales tends to dry out the straw and compost quickly. Daily watering of the straw and rooting soil is needed.

Roots develop very quickly and so long as they never lack moisture, the plants make vigorous growth. The usual method of supporting the plants is needed with individual canes or by string fixed to the rafters and round the plant stems. Since the bale sinks as it decomposes do not tie the plants too tightly. Ventilation is also important.

Once the first truss of fruits can be seen, give the plants liquid organic feeds every fourteen days. Choose a feed fairly high in potash since the decomposing straw will provide all the nitrogen needed. Another advantage from the decomposing straw is that there is an escape of carbon dioxide which aids the production of heavier crops.

Bale-grown plants are subject to pest attacks as well as air borne fungus spores, which means that they must be looked over frequently so that any disorders or pests can be dealt with before they gain a hold. No trouble should occur from root rot, verticillium or soil nematodes. Comparison tests have shown that bale culture properly carried out, does produce a heavier crop from healthier plants although extra time has to be given to the regular watering and feeding processes.

Once cropping has finished, the decomposed straw becomes an excellent source of humus-forming organic compost for forking into garden beds and borders and around fruit trees and bushes.

Apart from the use of straw bales, experiments have been made in growing tomatoes on shallower beds of straw, made of wads about 20 cm. in depth. These have shown that it is possible to obtain greater yields of early fruit through higher plant population in the green-house.

Among successful experiments made, is the planting of four rows of plants on straw wad beds 20 cm. deep and 1·4 m. wide. This works out at 35 cm. apart in and between the rows. To avoid overcrowding stop the plants in the two outer rows and keep side shoots removed, when the third truss of fruit has set. The two inner rows can be allowed to produce up to six or seven trusses.

Outdoor ring culture is carried out in the same way as for greenhouse plants, although it is helpful if the sides of the aggregate layer in the trenches prepared for the plants, are protected by boards or bricks to keep it in position. The aggregate is made up in the manner indicated earlier and the rings, filled with the appropriate compost, placed 38 to 45 cm. apart.

Some growers avoid wind or late frost damage by erecting hessian around the rows or cloches or other glass structures can be placed over individual plants. In this way an early crop can be produced. Supports should be given as soon as plants go into the rings and nothing is better than strong bamboo canes and green fillis although the square rose supports are quite satisfactory.

By whatever method tomatoes are grown the regular removal of side shoots is necessary and a watch kept for aphis and other pests. It is essential to encourage the first truss to set, otherwise the plants grow leggy. Apart from the necessity of a moist atmosphere if the plants or their supports are given a sharp tap when the flowers are opening it does help to distribute the pollen leading to fertilisation.

### The Tom-Bag

One of the latest successful methods of growing tomatoes is by the Tom-Bag system. The bags used contain tomato compost which is specially formulated to produce the right type of good firm close-jointed growth, with broad dark green leaves and well developed flower trusses. This Tomato Compost contains all the necessary major, minor and trace elements, both in available and slow release forms, and in the correct balance with the emphasis on potash, to give the tomato plants a good start and encourage the development of high quality sound firm fruit.

It is normal to grow four plants in each

standard bag of which the size is 1·10 m. long, 38 cm. wide and 15 cm. deep, for a long term heated crop, and five plants for short term or cold house growing five or six trusses.

Raise the tomatoes in the usual way and before planting 38 cm. apart, shake the compost evenly along the bag which should be placed level and square up the sides. To form a single row, lay the bags end to end. Cut out the panels along the dotted lines to form a mini-trough, leaving the cross-bands to support the sides.

Place the young plants with the minimum of firming. Water thoroughly to moisten *all* the compost in the bag. String plants (with a non-slip loop, tied around the stem below the first leaf) to the overhead wire, and twist plants round the string in a clockwise direction. Canes should *not* be driven through the bags. Horizontal wires at 30 cm. intervals are ideal. Well fed plants carry heavy crops and must be properly supported.

After about one week when the Tom-Bags have settled and taken their final shape, you can puncture three drainage holes along either side of the bag about 13 mm. above ground level. This is not necessary unless you are going away and need to leave a sump of water in the bottom.

Keep the compost adequately moist at all times and avoid extremes of feeding and watering, especially when the plants are carrying a heavy weight of fruit. Once established, daily watering will probably be necessary, this however depends on the situation of the plants. It should always be possible to squeeze water out of the compost. Throughout the summer a vigorous plant of 1 m. or more growing under good conditions, requires an average $1\frac{1}{2}$ to 2 pints of water daily.

Tomatoes are gross feeders, so commence feeding once the first truss of fruit has formed and continue with regular feeding until the last truss is half developed.

# CHAPTER EIGHT

# *Vegetables Under Glass*

**In the Greenhouse**

The majority of glasshouses are used for ornamental plants, but it is possible without inconvenience, to grow quite a nice selection of vegetables and to have them available when outside crops are scarce. It has long been known that the intensity and duration of daylight have a marked effect on the time taken by vegetable crops to reach maturity. This has to be taken into account when planning the sowing and planting times of suitable vegetables.

Lettuces are among the easiest to manage and may be sown from early autumn onwards, the earliest sowings being ready for cutting within ten to twelve weeks. Later sowings can be made to provide crops over a long period, in fact it is possible with the aid of a greenhouse or frame to have lettuce available throughout the year.

For heated houses suitable varieties are: Amplus, Greenheart, Cheshunt Early Giant, Kloek and Grand Rapids. The simplest way is to sow the seeds in boxes, and later prick off the seedlings into other boxes.

Even with the greatest care, the seedlings are bound to receive a slight check at the time of pricking off and a further one at the time the plants are moved to their final positions, when they are about 8 cm. tall. Some check can be avoided by sowing the seed very thinly in beds in the greenhouse and then making the one move when the plants are big enough to handle.

A suitable sowing temperature is 12 to 15°C. although after germination has occurred heat can be decreased to 10°C. Plenty of ventilation will induce sturdy growth.

Whether lettuces are being grown on the greenhouse floor or on the bench, the aim should be to space them at least 18 cm. apart each way.

Carrots can be grown with success in the warm greenhouse, the sowing period for the early varieties extending from autumn to spring. First sowings will be ready for pulling in the New Year. They grow best on light loamy, sandy soils having a good humus content. Fresh organic manures are best avoided unless incorporated into the soil some months beforehand.

Some gardeners 'chit' the seed. To do this, soak it in water for about twenty four hours before sowing, spread it on a sheet of glass and cover with a moist cloth. As soon as the seeds sprout, mix them with an equal quantity of fine sand which makes sowing easier.

Choice of varieties is important the best forcing varieties having sufficient, but not too many leaves. Among these are Early Nantes and Amsterdam Forcing. Turnip Early Snowball can be treated in the same way as carrots although the chitting is not needed. Use the roots while they are small.

Chicory is also worth growing in the cool greenhouse. Roots can be lifted from the open ground in autumn. Prepare them by cutting off the leaves 25 mm. above the crowns, as they are lifted. Shorten them to a uniform length of about 20 cm. Then cover with a mixture of clean, sandy loamy soil, free from stones. Some growers force chicory successfully under the benches of a greenhouse.

A reasonable degree of moisture should be present to give the chicory its bright appearance. After heeling in the roots, leave them for two weeks keeping them in darkness. Increase heat to 20°C. but after three days reduce it to 15°C and later to 12°C. After four or five weeks the heads or chicons, should be ready for cutting. Washing the heads prior to use, adversely affects their keeping qualities.

Radishes can be grown successfully under glass so long as there are adequate supplies of organic matter in the soil. A close, hot atmosphere promotes leaf growth at the expense of the root. Sow seed in deep boxes, glasshouse bench, or in the greenhouse 'floor' soil.

Moderate heat is necessary, and if the light is reasonably good, a temperature of 8 to 10°C will be suitable. Any attempt to force growth during dull weather will result in plenty of foliage but little 'bulb'. Watering the growing crop is normally unnecessary and undesirable, although it is advisable to apply sufficient moisture to the soil before sowing, so there is enough to carry the crop to maturity. Short-topped varieties are best, including the forcing strain of French Breakfast, Sparkler and other turnip-shaped varieties.

A few roots of mint can also be brought into the greenhouse for winter production. Grow these in boxes or large pots, or on the greenhouse floor. Lay the roots flat in little trenches about 8 cm. deep and start them under cool conditions. Once growth is seen breaking through the surface a temperature of 10 to 13°C. is suitable. A few fine mist sprays of water will provide the required atmosphere making it possible to cut shoots over a long period.

Rhubarb can be forced under the staging, darkness being necessary if this crop is to be a success. Lift the roots from outdoor beds in early winter. Many gardeners leave them exposed to a few frosts before housing. Pack them closely together, filling the spaces with loose soil as work proceeds. Then give a light watering to settle the soil around the roots. If a temperature around 8°C. is provided for a week or so, growth will soon commence.

Later, heat can be increased to 10°C. and subsequently to 15°C. Good varieties for forcing under the staging or in a darkened corner of the greenhouse, are Prince Albert, Victoria and Timperley Early. It takes five or six weeks from planting time until they are ready for pulling.

Seakale can be grown in the same way, although since the roots are much smaller, they can be forced in large pots or boxes. Darkness is essential, otherwise the blanched roots will be unpalatable.

Dwarf French beans can be grown in pots or boxes in the cool greenhouse. For this purpose it is best to use 23 to 25 cm. pots well crocked containing fairly rich compost. Fill the pots to three parts of their depth and space seven or eight beans around the edge of the pot covering them with 3 cm. of soil. Subsequently, the number of plants can be reduced to four or five.

Lightly syringe the plants at frequent intervals. This ensures the flowers set well and keeps down red spider. Once the pods have set it is a good plan to apply liquid manure at ten day intervals. To keep the plants upright, place twiggy sticks in the pots. The aim should be to maintain a temperature of 12°C. or so, although no harm is done if it rises a little during the daytime. The plants appreciate fresh air but not draughts. Good varieties are Masterpiece and The Prince, both having long fleshy pods of good flavour.

Mustard and Cress can be sown in pots, boxes or on the greenhouse staging soil according to the quantity required. Sow little and often using a good compost made fairly firm and watered well. Do not cover with soil but apply brown paper to provide darkness, or stand the boxes in a dark position for a few days.

So that they mature together, sow cress four days before mustard. The latter will germinate within three or four days and both should be ready for cutting within seven or eight days.

Peas can be cultivated in pots or the greenhouse border. For pots, rely on dwarf varieties such as Kelvedon Wonder and Little Marvel which can be sown in winter for an early crop. The 25 cm. size pots will take six seeds. Sow them 40 mm. deep around the inside edge of clean, well crocked pots, filled to rather more than two-thirds of their depth, with a mixture of three parts good fibrous loam and one part each of leaf mould or peat and silver sand.

After sowing, water the pots and stand them on a shelf near the glass. As growth proceeds gradually fill the pots with more compost.

Avoid high temperatures keeping heat to 18°C. during the day with 5°C lower at night.

For border culture, provided the soil is good, fork over the ground, working in a dressing of bone meal at the rate of 3 or 4 oz. to the square metre. Sow in winter in drills about 4 cm. deep either in single rows or staggered. Provide twiggy sticks at an early stage and as growth develops suitable supports should be used.

Occasional overhead sprayings are beneficial. If the soil is moist before sowing it should not need watering very frequently. Keep the temperature from rising above 18°C.

Heated frames equipped with both soil warming and space heating, ought not to be left idle during the winter for they can be used to produce forced vegetables at little cost.

Make up the bed in the frame with care. If the intention is to force vegetables in pots or boxes, soil warming cables should be placed so that they are covered with 5 cm. of sand and the boxes placed on top. Where it is intended to grow plants in the soil bed in the frame, the cable must be covered with soil which is fine and good. The depth of the bed should ensure that the plants are near the glass without touching it. The roots must not come into contact with the electrical hot bed layer.

Once the bed is ready, the glazed lid should be placed on the frame for ten days or so. This will give weed seeds time to germinate. Leave the bed exposed to the weather for a week in order to get the soil thoroughly moistened. A few days after the lids have been replaced, switch on the current.

The following are among the crops which will succeed in a heated frame. Carrot, Amsterdam Forcing, of which seed should be sown in shallow drills 15 cm. apart and where the bed is 15 to 18 cm. deep. Thin the seedlings so they stand 5 to 8 cm. apart. Plenty of moisture and ventilation are needed. A day temperature of up to 15°C. is desirable. The crop should be ready from ten to twelve weeks after planting

### Making a hot bed

Frame beds provided with bottom heat will bring crops to maturity long before their normal season. Heat can be produced by using a mixture of animal manure and leaves. The origin of this method is based on the observation that a stacked heap of fermenting dung becomes very warm.

Fresh stable manure containing a proportion of straw provides the greatest degree of heat over the longest period. Although horse manure is not plentiful and to buy is expensive, it is ideal for raising early plants such as cabbages, cauliflowers, carrots, leeks, marrows, radishes, melons and similar subjects. Aubergines and sweet corn can also be raised on a hot bed where a greenhouse is not available. Hot beds cool off gradually and this encourages the production of sturdy plants which seldom run to seed.

The site chosen for the bed should be sheltered from cold winds with a water supply fairly near. Although beds can be made on normal ground level, if soil is taken out for about 30 cm. the bed will retain heat better. This should not be done on heavy ground, or in such positions where water is liable to drain.

The idea is to build a flat topped heap of well trodden manure at least 60 cm. high. A good mixture consists of three quarters of manure and a quarter of leaves well mixed together. This can be relied on to produce a temperature of 15 to 17°C. for a period of five or six weeks. If fresh manure is scarce use equal parts of fresh and old manure and leaves. These will produce a temperature of 10 to 12°C. lasting for seven or eight weeks. Liquid manure added to the heap will increase the heat.

After the heap has been well trodden down it should be watered if the manure is dry and boards to form the frame erected. The beds should overlap the boards by 8 cm. all round.

Wait a few days before putting on the frame lights to allow ammonia fumes to escape. Before doing so, place a layer of good fine soil on top of the heap. It is into this that the seeds will be sown. The heat from the rotting manure and leaves warms the soil and is trapped by the frame lights, so turning the frame into a little 'hothouse'.

Sowing can be done about six days after the lights are put on. As a means of retaining heat for a longer period, fresh horse manure can be placed against the outside boards.

*Using Tent Cloches for protection and early development of seedlings.*

## Cloche Gardening

Cloches represent a substantial capital outlay and the gardener will want to recover the initial cost of the cloches over a short period and to obtain full value from the crops grown. This can only be achieved if the cloches are usefully employed during most of the year.

Time and labour are the principal factors in the cost of production and it is important that as little time as possible should be spent in moving the cloches from one crop to another. This is most likely to be managed if the rows from which they are to be removed are close to the rows of the next crop.

To meet this requirement strip cropping should be practiced. The ground is divided into strips approximately 1·20 m. wide, each strip being separated from the next by a 60 cm. wide pathway.

In two strip cropping, the strips are grouped in pairs and the cloches are moved from one strip to the next and then back again. In three strip cropping, the strips are grouped in threes and the cloches either shuttled backwards and forwards, as in the two strip system, or moved on and on until they reach the end of the plot.

The latter method involves the transfer of a whole row of cloches from one end of the plot to the other. Two strip cropping is probably the best for the gardener who has only a moderate amount of ground under cloches and, for the space occupied, normally gives a better return.

133

This sytem requires rather more precise conditions, for seasonal weather may upset pre-arranged sowing and cropping dates.

The three strip system is more complex to plan in theory, but more elastic in practice, since it is never necessary to clear one crop in great haste to start another on the same strip.

With short rows, the strip system is unsuitable and should be replaced by the block system in which the cloches are moved from blocks on the left hand side of a central path, to blocks on the right hand side.

Although it is possible to plan and scheme timetables for strip rotations, it is not always convenient to follow those which have been worked out, under different conditions.

It is in the gardeners interest to grow crops which are wanted in the kitchen and will be ready when shop prices are at their highest, that is, two or three weeks before the outdoor supplies come along. Barn and tent type cloches are easily transported and moved from one place to another without dismantling.

Lettuce from the crop cloched in the late autumn should be ready for cutting in April. These can be followed by a late spring or early summer crop, such as sweet corn, marrows, French beans or turnips.

The growing of plants under cloches needs careful planning and management, and the need for correct timing of sowings and plantings is greater than for sowing on open land. This makes for greater efficiency and full cropping. Since glass promotes rapid growth, and enables more crops to be grown on a given piece of land in one season, the demands on soil fertility are higher, therefore manuring and especially organic manuring, to improve soil structure and general fertility has to be generous.

It is unwise to try to make a success of intensive production using cloches, unless the gardener is prepared in the first place to apply adequate amounts of animal manure or good substitutes. Main crops can be supplemented by catch crops and intercrops, provided that these do not unduly complicate the rotation.

Some gardeners favour the practice of using elevated cloches so that they can finish off late growing crops. Although this may only advance maturity by a few days, it does definitely improve quality.

## Strip Cropping

Various types of individual cloches have been in use for many years but with the introduction of continuous cloches it became possible to practice strip-cropping. This saves the somewhat laborious job of constantly moving cloches from one site to another: it also keeps them in regular use, and does away with the necessity of stacking at various times.

Strip-cropping consists in dividing up the ground to be cultivated into strips of equal width. In two-strip cropping there are two adjacent strips and in three-strip cropping, three different sites for the crops. The width of the sites will depend on the type of cloches used. On, say a strip 6 ft. wide, there would be room for two rows and a pathway.

A number of crops can be sown directly under cloches, others will be raised in warmth and then planted in strips, whilst in some instances the cloches will be moved from one crop to another during the growing season, or be used to give protection prior to harvesting.

Although the crops to be grown will naturally depend on personal requirements, and the cloches can be used according to these needs, the following are examples of easily manageable rotational coverings.

# Two-Strip Rotations for Cloches

## Strip One

1. *October—April*
Lettuce
*June—September*
Frame cucumbers

2. *October—April*
Lettuce intercropped with peas.
*June—September*
Melons

*April—June*
Tomatoes or aubergines
*April—May*
Radishes

## Strip Two

*April—June*
Dwarf beans
*September—November*
Lettuce (sown in August)

*April—June*
Tomatoes
*September—October*
Tomatoes on straw for ripening

3. *January—April*
Lettuce & Early Carrots
*June—October*
Late tomatoes

## Three-Strip Rotations

### Strip One

1. *October—April*
Lettuce

2. *November—March*
Spring cabbage

### Strip Two

*April—May*
Marrows

*March—April*
Cauliflowers

### Strip Three

*June—September*
Melons

*April—July*
Dwarf beans

These dates will vary in different parts of the country and according to weather conditions. Two-strip cropping is simpler to manipulate than the three-strip method. It is easier to move the cloches, with a shorter distance to carry them.

# Crop Rotation

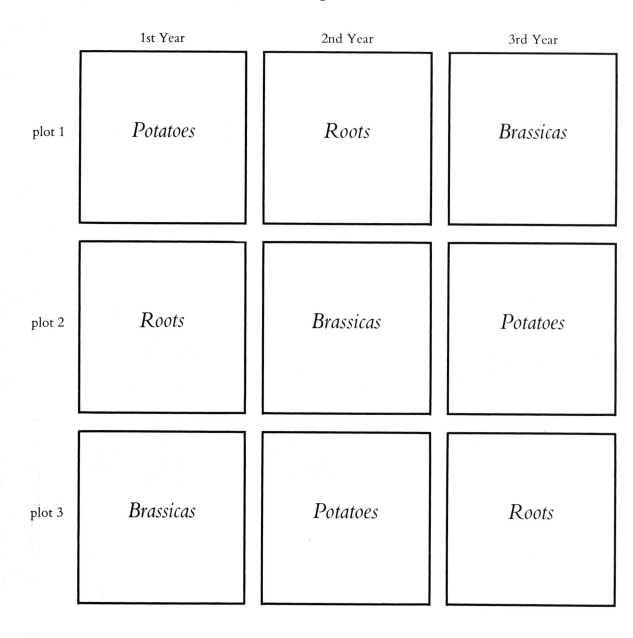

|  | 1st Year | 2nd Year | 3rd Year |
|---|---|---|---|
| plot 1 | *Potatoes* | *Roots* | *Brassicas* |
| plot 2 | *Roots* | *Brassicas* | *Potatoes* |
| plot 3 | *Brassicas* | *Potatoes* | *Roots* |

# CHAPTER NINE

# Storing, Preserving and Freezing Vegetables

*Left to right: Peas, Runner beans, Onions, Beetroot, Carrots, early Potatoes, Cabbages (summer), Brussels sprouts* Vegetable Plot *(1)*

## Successional Sowings

However carefully a cropping plan is prepared, there are nearly always times when there is a glut of vegetables and other periods when they are in very short supply. This is where the correct storage of vegetables can be of great help in ensuring regular supplies.

It is possible to store certain root vegetables so that they last in first class condition for many months. This applies in particular to such items as potatoes, beetroot and carrots. As far as potatoes are concerned, the usual method is to 'clamp' them for winter and spring use. The

fairly common practice of keeping the tubers in a warm room or heated garage is unwise, for it induces the early growth of shoots, shrivelling and loss of flavour.

Potatoes intended for storing should be thoroughly dried off before they are bagged or clamped. Any showing signs of disease or damage should not be kept. Even one or two diseased tubers will cause a large proportion of the crop to decay. Whilst comparatively small quantities can be stored in boxes, using a layer of soil or sand between each row of roots, large quantities are best stored in clamps or

*Left to right: Brussels sprouts, Cabbages (spring),
Peas, Runner beans, Onions, Beetroot, Carrots, early
Potatoes*   Vegetable Plot *(2)*

'pies', as they are sometimes known.

To make a clamp the first essential is to select a site which is dry and not likely to be flooded in winter. For this reason a place rather higher than the surrounding ground-level should be chosen. First give the base of the site a good dusting of lime and then put down straw to a depth of 4 in. (10 cm.) After this the heaping of the tubers can be commenced.

It is usual to make the clamp more or less round, but in the case of really large quantities, a long ridge-shaped heap up 1 m. high, can be made. After the potatoes have been carefully heaped, a 13 to 15 cm. layer of straw should be placed over the tubers and an air vent filled

with straw left to allow for sweating.

When there is the likelihood of frost, a layer of soil should be placed over the straw. At first this can be about 15 cm. thick, but as the weather becomes cooler, and according to the district, more soil will be needed. In most cases the soil can be obtained by digging a trench around the clamp and throwing this on to the heap. Press it down firmly and smoothly, beating it tightly so that rain is thrown off and does not seep on to the tubers.

The twisted tufts of straw used in the ventilators will carry off moisture and prevent overheating. In late winter open the clamp occasionally, to make sure the tubers are not

*Left to right: Beetrot, Carrot, early Potatoes, Brussels sprouts, Cabbages (spring), Peas, Runner beans, Onions* Vegetable Plot *(3)*

decaying. Make sure that the ends are resealed properly, otherwise frost may damage some of the tubers.

When storing beetroot and carrots pack the roots in alternate layers, shoulders facing one way and tapering roots the other. Beetroot must not have their tops cut, these should be twisted off before being stored. If they are cut they 'bleed' and become useless.

Onions do not need elaborate frost protection. They must be thoroughly dried off and this is best done by placing them on raised wire netting to allow free circulation of air.

There are various methods of storing the bulbs but they should not be kept in a warm room. One good way is to keep them in old nylon stockings partially filled and hung up in a frostproof shed. They can be layed out in trays which are stored on top of each other. This certainly saves space. Finally there is the rope storage method. This can be quite elaborate but the quick way is to tie the onions on to a stout cord by their own half withered tops. The complete twist of the onion around the cord keeps them in position. Start with the bigger onions at the base finishing with the smaller ones at the top. A strong rope holding 12 ot 15 lb. is quite satisfactory.

Apart from root vegetables such as potatoes,

*Carrots for storage*

carrots, beetroots, etc., which can be stored in clamps, boxes or large pots, there are some vegetables which can be preserved for winter use. In many gardens there is a glut during the summer and very irregular and insufficient supplies for the household during the winter. The latter period is, of course, the one in which vegetables are most expensive to purchase and this in itself should be a real incentive to provide crops during the time when to buy, runs away with the money. Much can and should be done to ensure that vegetables are available during the winter and early spring, and thus improve the economic situation.

Obviously fresh vegetables are limited, but the growing of certain subjects for preserving is a worthwhile venture. While many root crops such as beetroot, carrots and onions can be stored in boxes or clamps, the flavour of bottled vegetables has to be tasted to be appreciated. Nearly all of us grow more than we can use when a crop is at its best and this is another reason why the preservation of vegetables ought to be more widely practised. Perhaps the most important thing to remember in this connection is that vegetables must be gathered and bottled the same day.

What then, are the subjects which respond well to this treatment? There are a number, including Green Windsor broad beans and runner beans, which, if bottled when young and tender, are, I think, better than when salted. Beetroot, new potatoes, which can be a real treat at Christmas time, rhubarb and tomatoes. While the latter may not be a vegetable it is usually served as one when it has been preserved.

An additional row of onions of the pickling variety should certainly be grown and a few extra celery plants should be put in, so that the hearts of these can be bottled. Young asparagus crowns also bottle well and cauliflowers must definitely be included for pickling purposes. Thinking of pickles, a few seeds of capsicums should be sown in pots and planted out later. They will provide the 'hotness' to go with the cauliflowers and onions.

Where a pressure cooker is available peas should definitely be included in the preserving programme, so that an extra row or two should be sown for this purpose. When we come to dwarf beans for storing, there is an attractive choice to grow. The food value of these is very high and they require exactly the same culture as the more usual varieties. Comtesse de Chambord is small, white and of good flavour. Brown Dutch is bigger and an attractive orange-brown shade. Then there is the black bean, Mexican Black, which is of good flavour. The Czar is a runner of the butter-bean type, with large white seeds.

A few marrows should also be grown for storing purposes, while, of course, care should be taken to ensure that the more usual 'keeping' roots are so stored that they do not deteriorate before they can be used.

**Vegetables For The Freezer**
Apart from the cost of buying fresh vegetables when garden supplies have become exhausted, it often happens that at certain times there is such an abundance of home grown vegetables available that they cannot all be used immediately. This is where the home freezer provides a solution.

This is not the place to go into the full details of preparation and blanching since such information is usually supplied by the freezer manufacturer. The first consideration is to select finest quality specimens in a young condition and wich can be prepared and frozen immediately they are gathered. Never allow the vegetables to remain in the sun or a warm position or they will wilt and lose their flavour. Make sure too, they are clean and that no damaged specimens are used.

After preparation put the vegetables into the freezer immediately and once they are frozen, place them in a bag which should be sealed and returned to the freezer.

Some vegetables respond to the freezing treatment better than others, while certain varieties of the same subject 'come out' better. The following have proved to be very suitable if prepared well and there are others worth trying.

*Asparagus.* Mary Washington, Connovers Colossal. Choose young spears of even size 15 cm. long.

*Broad Beans.* Green Longpod, White Longpod. Make sure to pick young.

*French or Snap Beans.* Masterpiece, Tendercrop, Flair.

*Runner Beans.* Scarlet Emperor, Kelvedon Marvel. Trim and string.

*Beetroot.* Detroit and other globe varieties. Not the long kinds.

*Broccoli.* White and purple sprouting. Green sprouting or Calabrese.

*Brussels Sprouts.* Peer Gynt, King Arthur and Stabilo. Choose firm compact specimens.

*Carrots.* Chantenay, Early Nantes. Select young firm roots.

*Cauliflowers.* Snowball, Majestic, Dominant, All the Year Round.

*Celery,* white. Loses its crispness when frozen, but useful for cooking. Select fresh young hearts.

*Corn on the Cob.* Kelvedon Glory, Xtra-Sweet. Make sure to pull off husk and silk.

*Courgettes.* Select young firm specimens about 10 to 15 cm. long.

*Egg Plant.* Aubergine Long Purple will freeze successfully if good sized firm fruits are used before they grow old.

*Florence Fennel.* The bulbous roots can be treated the same as celery. Both have similar aniseed-like flavour.

*Lettuce.* These are reasonably successful when frozen. Make sure to select soft, (not tough and stringy) quickly grown specimens.

*Marrows* can be frozen so long as the young bush type are used.

*Mushrooms* are usually available fresh throughout the year but a few could be placed in the deep freeze. There is no need for blanching.

*Peas.* Little Marvel, Gradus and Petit Pois can be used, as can the Sugar Pea and other Mange Tout types. All should be gathered while young.

*Peppers* or capsicums, green and red are worth freezing when plentiful.

*Potatoes.* Small even specimens should be chosen from varieties such as Home Guard or Majestic. Lightly cook and cut chips or make up potato croquettes when cold; pack in bags and freeze.

*Root crops* including parsnips, turnips and swedes store well but if convenient, a small quantity can be frozen, first being cooked and cubed before packing into containers. Onions should be kept separate otherwise their odour may contaminate other foods.

*Spinach,* perpetual, prickly and New Zealand all freeze well. Select young undamaged leaves, removing thick stems and coarse mid-ribs.

*Tomatoes.* Use firm, just ripe fruits of medium size. While they can be frozen whole or halved, so they can be used for grilling, some of the flavour is lost. It is better to make tomato puree. For this, peel and cut up the fruits quickly, otherwise they become a watery product. When taken out of the freezer remember to season the puree before serving.

## Sowing vegetables for succession

The problem of maintaining a continuity of supply can be largely overcome by selecting varieties which mature at different times even though they may be sown or planted on the same day.

There is considerable variation in the time some varieties take to reach maturity. Many vegetables seed catalogues give information on this point.

Because of their quick growth, early varieties are also used for late summer sowings for maturing before winter sets in. Among the advantages of early varieties is their good flavour, and the fact that they escape the attack of pests and diseases which seem to strike more often at mid-season and late crops.

Four of the most important vegetables are cabbages, carrots, peas and potatoes and of all of these there are early, mid-season and late varieties.

Cabbages can be sown from spring to autumn. The so-called spring maturing cabbages come from early autumn sowings. Quick maturing cabbages from spring sowings include Golden Acre. Those for winter harvesting include Christmas Drumhead and the so called ballhead varieties of which seed can be sown in succession.

Carrots mature at different times, and extra early varieties can be sown in frames from late winter until early summer to be followed by the large varieties of the half-long and long types, which are excellent for storing in boxes or clamps.

Peas are grouped in the same way, and should be sown in succession. First early varieties need eight to twelve weeks from sowing to maturity. Second early twelve to thirteen weeks and main crops thirteen to fifteen weeks. Because the maincrops take so long to mature they should not be sown after mid-summer. From that time it is best to go back to the First Early sorts since these take so much less time to grow. The only danger here is the possibility of mildew.

Potatoes too can be planted to provide a long succession of tubers. First early varieties should be planted in early spring, earlier in warmer districts or where frames are being used. This should then secure tubers from early summer onwards. These are followed by second earlies. The maincrop varieties are used for storing and these normally produce the heaviest yields.

*Beetroot Detroit Globe*, having blood-red uniform flesh and fine grained texture, can be sown throughout the summer.

*Dwarf French beans* such as Masterpiece which makes bushy plants with long, sturdy tender pods can be sown early in the greenhouse, where there is gentle heat both in spring and early autumn. Outdoor sowings can be made in spring and early summer. Longpod broad beans sown outdoors in autumn, will mature in early spring, while the Windsor strains are best for spring sowing.

*Brussels Sprouts* can be sown in a cold frame in late summer for maturing the following summer rather than the autumn, which is the usual time for sprouts. These are supplemented by the outdoor early spring sowings. Cauliflower All the Year Round can also be sown in summer for wintering in well ventilated frames.

*Cress curled*. For continuous supplies, successive sowings can be made under glass throughout the autumn and early winter.

*Endive Green Curled* too, can be sown in summer choosing a sheltered place and blanching the plants with large flower pots or after tying the leaves together, to keep out light.

*Spinach* such as the Giant Leaved Winter and Spinach Beet, sown in summer should provide a good winter picking, as will turnips, including Golden Ball which forms succulent roots. Hardy Green and Seven Top are grown for their tops, which make a good substitute for other types of greens.

*Garden Swedes* including Purple Top and Bronze Top are reliable sorts while another named Chignecto, has been bred for resistance to club root. All are excellent winter and early spring vegetables.

The cropping season can be still further extended by the use of cloches. Actual dates of cloching and decloching will vary in the north and south of the country while allowance must be made for climatic differences.

In addition to the normal coverage of a single crop, a two strip or three strip system of rotation is practiced, since it is not necessary to keep the cloches over particular crops until they mature. Examples of suggested strip coverings will be found in the Chapter on growing under glass.

# CHAPTER TEN

# *Diseases and Pests*

As Sir Robert Carrison said in Nutrition and Health, 'impoverishment of the soil leads to a whole train of evils; pasture of poor quality, poor quality of stock raised on it, poor quality of vegetables that man cultivates for himself, and faulty nutrition that results in disease in both man and beast.'

It is easy to use modern pesticides and destroy not only the pests but the invaluable predators as well. Every serious organic gardener knows that a healthy soil is conducive to healthy plant growth with a natural resistance to pests and disorders.

While we cannot prevent the appearance of all pests, we can co-operate with nature, taking such action as will destroy plant enemies without using poisonous sprays which will kill friend and foe and even spoil the flavour of the crop too.

Much can be done in the way of securing good crops free from pests and diseases by a system of rotation. This means that the same crop does not occupy a particular site more than a year or two. It is a help in securing produce of good quality if subjects and varieties known to succeed in particular types of soil and areas are grown.

Where there has been trouble with specific diseases it is best to grow other varieties not so susceptible.

Many insecticides and fungicides have unforeseen side effects which may prove more harmful than the original trouble. Many of the sprays kill predators which keep down harmful pests. Some will kill bees. Systemic sprays are now widely used. These are taken up into the sap and can remain poisonous to some useful insects for several days. Ladybirds, among the most valuable of aphis predators, are regularly and needlessly destroyed. More of these voracious feeders are needed, yet they seem to be getting scarcer.

There is a tendency for some gardeners to kill everything, insects or birds, wherever they are seen. Slugs and snails, greenfly, blackfly and white or grey fly should never be spared, but others including birds do a tremendous amount of good in the vegetable garden. As the number of predators decrease, so more pests survive.

While it is true that large numbers of pests and diseases *can* attack vegetables, crops grown on organic lines, where the humus content of the soil is high, and where the soil, and not simply the crops has been fed, are much less likely to be attacked or succumb to disorders.

Correctly treated soil results in healthy growth, able to withstand attacks from pests and diseases much better than ill nourished, poorly developed crops. This is not speculation or imagination, but a fact that is being proved by an ever increasing number of organic gardeners in many different parts of the world.

Fertile soil well supplied with organic matter ensures that crops receive adequate, constant supplies of feeding matter including inorganic minerals. Therefore they do not suffer from deficiency diseases or conditions associated with such shortages.

It would be foolish to suggest that an organic soil alone will ensure good, well flavoured crops. For proper growth, plants also need light, air, room to develop, and the right rooting conditions including soil aeration and

## Pests commonly found in the U.S.A.

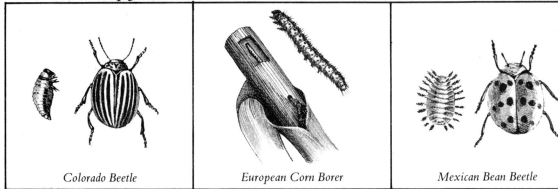

Colorado Beetle

European Corn Borer

Mexican Bean Beetle

## Pests commonly found in Europe and U.S.A.

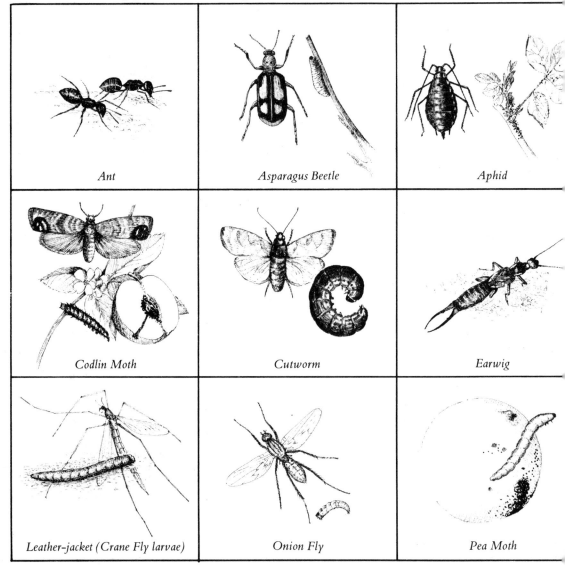

Ant

Asparagus Beetle

Aphid

Codlin Moth

Cutworm

Earwig

Leather-jacket (Crane Fly larvae)

Onion Fly

Pea Moth

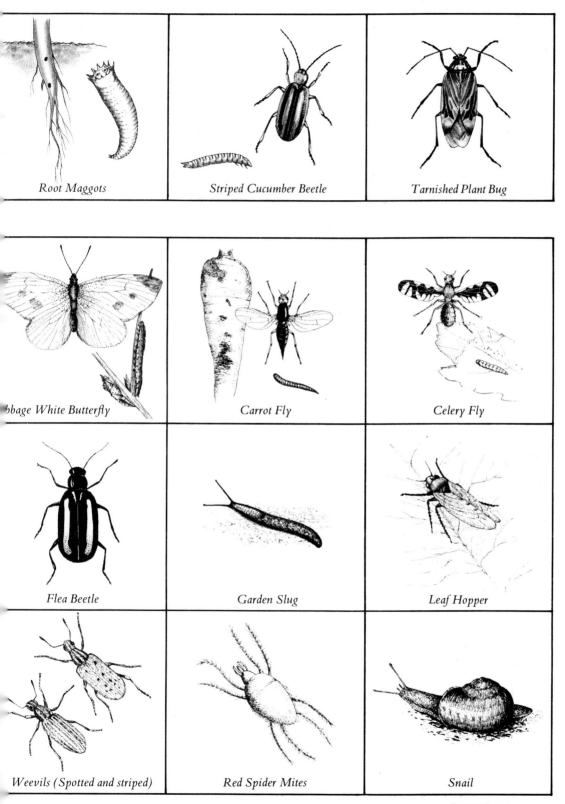

*Root Maggots*

*Striped Cucumber Beetle*

*Tarnished Plant Bug*

*...bbage White Butterfly*

*Carrot Fly*

*Celery Fly*

*Flea Beetle*

*Garden Slug*

*Leaf Hopper*

*Weevils (Spotted and striped)*

*Red Spider Mites*

*Snail*

*Continued overleaf*

good drainage, with of course, sufficient moisture.

As we have seen earlier, crop rotation and growing crops suited to particular soils do help to secure good results. It is not practicable to change from being an orthodox gardener to the organic method in one season, and this is why it is necessary to dwell on pests and diseases at a greater length than is needed by the established organic gardener.

One way in which the grower can help himself (or herself) is to buy first-class seeds.

Compost grown seeds are still not as plentiful as one would like, but strains from well known sources can usually be depended upon.

There is no doubt that seeds do inherit some of the qualities, both good and bad, of their parents, so that the right stocks are of importance although the latest re-selected strains of some subjects are not necessarily better as far as flavour and productivity are concerned.

It is possible to spend more money on pesticides than the cost of buying vegetables, but there is no need to use expensive remedies

## Pests and Diseases

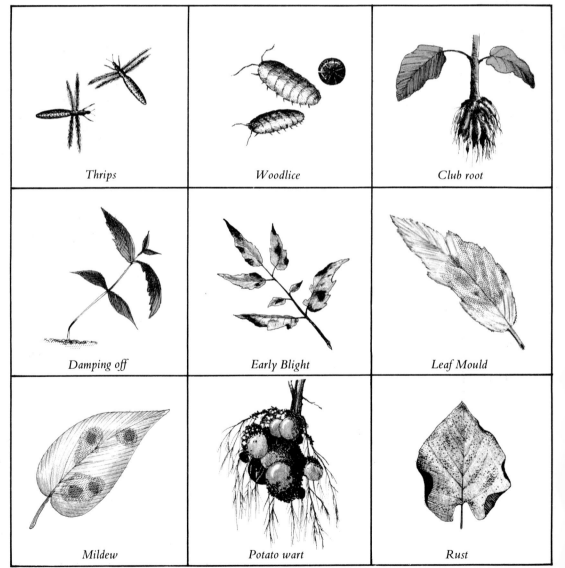

| | | |
|---|---|---|
| *Thrips* | *Woodlice* | *Club root* |
| *Damping off* | *Early Blight* | *Leaf Mould* |
| *Mildew* | *Potato wart* | *Rust* |

for there are many safe and effective ways of avoiding invaders of which the following are likely to be the chief.

**Ants.** Although they do not cause direct damage to plants, ants can loosen the roots with their nesting operations. They are attracted to the honey-dew secreted by aphids and will swarm over infested plants. Derris and pyrethrum dusts are effective killers, while a Pidero solution poured into the nests will destroy.

**Asparagus Beetle.** These pests lay their eggs on growing shoots in June and develop into greyish grubs which feed on the foliage and then burrow into the soil. There, they either turn into beetles or remain in the soil until the following spring. Spraying the plants with liquid derris or Pidero will destroy these pests.

**Black Fly** attacks many subjects and the aim should be to destroy them as soon as seen, otherwise they increase rapidly.

To avoid black fly on broad beans, sow long pods in the autumn, for then flowers appear and pods set before the flies arrive. Nip out growing points if the flies are seen. In bad areas, grow only Early Longpods avoiding Windsors until June for autumn cropping.

Compost the plants as soon as the crop is finished or late shoots will harbour flies. Make sure flies are not breeding in beetroot, spinach, nasturtiums and other annuals, or on weeds such as fat hen. Euonymus hedges should be sprayed with a tar oil wash in winter.

**Cabbage Aphis.** This is often harboured on winter cabbages or old brassica stumps which should always be removed. Derris and pyrethrum sprays will usually keep plants clean although spraying early before the pests are fully active is advisable.

**Cabbage caterpillar and white butterfly** of which there are large and small species. Nicotine can be used in the early stages of growth but not nearer than four or five weeks from time of cutting, when liquid derris or Pidero should be depended upon, alternatively, stir $\frac{1}{4}$ lb. common salt into 2 gallons of water and spray the plants.

**Cabbage Root Fly.** The old-fashioned method of using 13 to 15 cm. squares of tarred felt is still one of the best remedies. A hole is made in the centre through which the root of the plant is pushed before being put into the soil. Do this in May and June or try a pinch of naphthalene at base of each plant.

**Cabbage White Butterfly** see Cabbage Caterpillar.

**Cabbage Whitefly.** This is a most disfiguring pest showing as clouds of small flies when the plants are disturbed. They affect all members of the brassica family and since there are several generations each season they should be dealt with early.

Spray the undersides of leaves where the flat egg-like larvae will be found and destroy the lower, older, discoloured leaves, since it is from these the subsequent broods hatch. Spray with nicotine wash some weeks before the eating stage, otherwise dissolve $\frac{3}{4}$ lb. soft soap in two gallons of water and spray the plants thoroughly two or three times.

**Carrot Fly.** This pest is guided by the scent of the foliage, which should never be rubbed or bruised. Masking the scent will only apply at certain times, particularly May and June. Growing onions between rows of carrots will often keep the fly away, as will paraffin sprinkled on sand around the plants, or try stretching creosoted cord or placing the scented pine sawdust along the rows.

**Celery Fly** (and leafminer). This attacks celery, parsnips and parsley. The fly lays its eggs during spring and summer on the upper side of the leaves. Tiny legless maggots hatch out and enter the leaves where they feed, producing blisters. Affected leaves should be removed and burned. Naphthalene dusted along the rows, or rags dipped in paraffin hung near the plants prevents the fly from laying her eggs.

**Cutworms.** These are the caterpillar of the Turnip Moth, Agrostis segetam. They cause damage to many plants by feeding on the leaves and stems at ground level. Their habit of biting through the stems gives them their common name. The moths lay their eggs at the base of the plants and the caterpillars feed at night. Frequent cultivation keeps these pests down, or naphthalene can be worked into the soil where they are known to occur.

**Earwigs** are not a serious menace in the vegetable garden and they do eat some pests. They sometimes feed on leaves. Vegetable traps or sawdust under an upturned flower pot will catch them, while Pidero will kill them on contact.

**Eelworms.** These are microscopic eel-like creatures which feed on the root or leaf tissues causing distortion and discolouration. Lettuce, tomatoes and potatoes on which they form cysts are the most likely to be affected. Crop rotation lessens the possibility of these pests and with hygienic cultivation they need not become a menace. Digging in mustard plants as green manure and keeping the soil rich in humus matter lessens the possibility of eelworm appearing.

**Flea Beetle.** These jumping insects attack seedlings and young plants of all members of the brassica family, riddling their leaves with small circular holes. They flourish under dry conditions and it is wise to keep up the humus content of the soil since this holds moisture at times of drought when the beetles increase rapidly. Weeds such as Shepherds Purse and Charlock should be kept down, since these can act as breeding places. Derris dusted along the rows at the time seedlings are emerging will normally destroy the pests.

**Greenfly.** Like all aphids, these are easily destroyed but most of the usual remedies kill the predators including Ladybirds, the gardeners friend. Pidero is one of the best proprietory greenfly killers and with derris and pyrethrum can be used anywhere in the garden. Quassia, that old-fashioned garden pest killer, is both effective and cheap. It is easy to make by boiling 4 oz. of chips in a gallon of water for two hours. Pour off the yellow liquid when cool and dilute with five parts of water. It will kill both aphids and small caterpillars. An alternative is to boil 3 lbs. of cut up rhubarb leaves in 3 quarts of water for three hours. Then dissolve 1 oz. soap flakes in a quart of water and mix it in the rhubarb water and use as an aphis spray.

**Leather-jackets.** These are the larvae of the Crane fly or Daddy-Long-Legs. It feeds on the roots of lettuce, brassicas and grass during spring and summer. The larvae can be controlled by watering with derris or Pidero in early autumn or naphthalene 2 oz. to the square metre will destroy these pests.

**Lettuce root aphis** can be very destructive. It is most prevalent in warm weather when attacked plants rapidly wilt and die. This pest often migrates from poplar trees and also attacks various weeds including sow thistles and fat hen. They attack the roots which when lifted reveal yellowish aphids hiding in a white wool-like substance. Any lettuce plants which suddenly wilt should be suspected and the entire row thoroughly soaked with liquid derris.

**Millipedes.** These are troublesome soil pests which can do much damage and although there are various proprietary pesticides, the simplest way is to make traps of portions of root crops such as cabbage or potatoes and to bury these in small perforated tins or impale them on a pointed stick. These traps can be examined at frequent intervals and the pests destroyed.

**Moles.** These are sometimes a problem and although they can be destroyed by using the special mole traps, many gardeners do not like doing this. In such cases the use of Torvil can be recommended. This is a kind of smoke, the fumes of which keep the moles away but does not kill them. Carbon monoxide or Moth balls can be placed in the runs, while Euphorbia lathyrus is sometimes grown since the root secretion emitted is known to drive moles away, but not kill them.

**Onion Fly.** This pest lays its eggs in the bulbs in spring and early summer. The scent of the crop makes it easy for the fly to find the bulbs. Eggs are sometimes laid on the side of the bulbs or even on the leaves, there, they hatch and burrow into the plant, eventually changing to a pupae which turns into flies. The foliage of infested bulbs becomes very pale and the bulbs a pulpy mass, containing many maggots. Growing onions from sets instead of seed lessens the possibility of attack but onion foliage should not be bruised since it is the scent which attracts the flies, which seem more likely to attack where manure and nitrogenous fertilisers are used rather than compost.

**Pea and Bean Weevils.** These damage leaves, especially of young plants by eating round the edges in a fairly regular way. They are less likely to attack healthy, steadily growing plants. Dusting the foliage when dry with derris or soot is usually sufficient to prevent further damage.

**Potato Eelworm** is microscopic in size, forming brown cysts containing clusters of the pests. Attacked plants become dwarfed and sickly-looking, with pale leaves and few tubers. This pest also attacks weeds including the woody nightshade which then become host plants. Eelworm is much less likely to occur in soils having a high humus content and there is now a predatory fungi which lives in humus and attacks and destroys eelworm. Another method is to grow tagetes, which experiments show have an adverse effect on eelworm as they do on other pests.

**Red Spiders** are very tiny mites which live by sucking the sap of plants. They attack cucumbers, melons and greenhouse plants, but can only flourish under dry conditions. A derris or soft soap solution will destroy these creatures.

**Slugs.** Apart from using proprietory brands of slug bait, these pests can be caught by placing saucers of sweetened water or beer in places where the pests are known to hide. They can also be caught in pieces of vegetable buried in the soil. This means that they have to be removed, which is not a difficult matter. One advantage of this method is that the dead slugs are not poisonous to birds as they are if some of the slug poisons are employed. Soot or crushed egg shells sprinkled around plants act as a deterrent.

**Snails.** These breed and increase in damp rubbish and under very low growing shrubs or leafy plants. Proprietory slug baits will usually destroy snails although it is best to avoid those which are poisonous since they may kill beneficial birds which often feed on snails.

**Wireworms** which are the larvae of the Click Beetle are most troublesome on newly cultivated land, specially where there has been grass. They can be dealt with as recommended for millipedes.

**Woodlice.** These are more a problem in the greenhouse than in the open ground. They breed most freely where rubbish is left lying about or where portions of dead or decaying trees are in the vicinity. The remedy is obvious, although there are a number of woodlice proprietory killers. They are also attracted to the traps suggested for the slugs.

**Whitefly.** There are several species of these. They settle on many kinds of outdoor and indoor plants. Under glass, using the white fly parasite Encarsia formosa, is a reliable and rapid way of getting rid of the pest but outdoors, the parasite would only be effective in July and August. Petroleum emulsion is useful, but should be used well in advance of the vegetables being eaten. Liquid derris or Quassia Extract will restrict the creatures but does not always eradicate them. Removing the larvae from the lower leaves of brassicas helps to control the menace.

Natural pest killers should be encouraged in the garden. Of these hedgehogs are most valuable. Saucers of milk or water placed in easily accessible corners helps them to be friendly. Unfortunately, they can be harmed or killed if they eat lots of slugs which have been poisoned by various slug baits.

Toads too, are useful. Blue Tits can often be seen busily clearing pests from plants and trees, while ladybirds are a real help to the gardener. There are also several parasitic wasps which should be encouraged, as well as the Lacewing and the Hover Fly.

**DISEASES**

There are two types of plant disease, the most common being those caused by a pathological organism and which are transmissible, and those brought about by physiological conditions and which do not spread from one plant to another. Diseases must be identified so that the correct diagnosis can be made and the right remedy is applied.

Transmissible disorders are mainly caused by fungi, bacteria or virus. Fungi live on living tissues as well as decaying and dead matter. They flourish under warm, humid conditions, especially where the attacked plant is growing poorly or is suffering from nutritional imbalance. Fungi overwinter in various ways and then reappear in strength in spring.

The common grey mould, Botrytis cinerea, can spread rapidly as can the several forms of mildew. Downy mildew will cause stunting and deformity. Bacterial diseases cause spotting and rots as well as galls, particularly on members of the brassica family.

Virus disorders have become prominent during recent years and although the particles are small they multiply rapidly. Their presence in the foliage is often seen by the yellowing of the leaf veins or of the whole leaf, while the leaves may curl. Brown streaks or circles may also appear on the leaves while with a few subjects, virus can come through the seed but usually it is spread by actual contact between healthy and infected plants or by insects, particularly aphids and the ants which attack them.

To attempt to mention all the possible diseases which might occur in the garden could easily lead one to conclude that it is simply not worth growing vegetables at all. This is the feeling the gardener gets when he sees shops and markets showing so many so called remedies.

The organic grower knows that prevention is better than cure and that hygiene in the garden goes a long way in keeping disorders away.

Even so, reference to a few of the more likely diseases will help to identify them and enable immediate steps to be taken to deal with them.

**Anthracnose** is sometimes a nuisance on dwarf beans and occasionally runner beans. It shows itself in dark circular leaf spots, cankered stems and cratered pods. Reject seeds showing dark patches and spray suspected plants with half strength Bordeaux Mixture or a similar fungicide.

**Chocolate Spot.** This is a form of botrytis which attacks Broad Beans. This crop is best grown in sheltered positions in good well-fed soil. Spray early with Bordeaux Mixture. In bad cases, the plants should be destroyed.

**Club Root.** All brassicas, including turnips and swedes can be affected. Rotation of crops and the presence of lime in the soil lessens the strength of this evil smelling disease. Dusting Calomel in the root holes is effective, while dropping Mothballs into the dibber holes or several 3 in. long sections of rhubarb stem when planting, have had some success.

**Damping off.** This comes from a species of Pythium and is most likely to occur under damp, stuffy conditions and when young plants are crowded together. Affected plants must be removed. Avoid thick sowing.

**Halo Blight** is of bacterium origin affecting dwarf and runner beans. It shows an angular water soaked spots on the leaves which turn brown, as do the pods, the seeds becoming blistered. Do not sow blistered seeds and destroy affected plants when the crop has been gathered. Dwarf Bean The Prince, is a resistant variety.

**Onion White Rot.** Keep a watch for this disease which can soon spoil an entire row of plants. The leaves turn yellow and flag and a white fluffy mould develops at the base of the bulbs. As this ripens, it falls and reinfects the soil. Choose a fresh site for onions once the disease has occurred.

**Potato Scab.** This fungus produces rusty and slightly raised scabs on the tubers although quality is unaffected. Avoid planting scabby sets and before putting in the tubers, surround them with peat or leaf mould. Rotational cropping is advisable.

**Potato and Tomato Blight.** Affected leaves develop moist almost black blotches which spread until the whole haulm dies. The tubers decay and in the case of tomatoes, the fruit is occasionally affected before the leaves.

Keep the soil uniformly moist and spray early with a good fungicide such as Burgundy or Bordeaux Mixture.

**Rust on Mint** is due to a fungus. Affected plants are best destroyed since the orange–rusty spots soon weaken the plants. Propagate only clean healthy specimens.

**Tip Burn** appears chiefly on lettuces. It is a physiological condition, largely caused by an irregular intake of moisture, often being prevalent in a very dry season. Some varieties are resistant to the disorder.

**Physiological or non-transmissible diseases** occur for various reasons including climatic conditions, growth disturbance and where certain part of the plant is not functioning correctly. They are not caused by pests which is why they are sometimes difficult to identify.

**Lack of balanced feeding matter,** that is, nutrient deficiency, often produces peculiar symptoms such as foliage distortion, discoloration and the dying back of the shoots.

*Chief among these are:*

**Nitrogen deficiency.** To overcome this dress with soil, mixed with dried blood or hoof and horn meal, or apply liquid fertiliser with a high nitrogen content. The application of a fertiliser rich in phosphorus and potassium such as bone meal when the ground is being turned over, is helpful.

**Phosphorus deficiency** is seen in slow growth and deep green almost purplish foliage. Here again bone meal is helpful.

**Calcium deficiency** shows in the foliage becoming anaemic-looking. Apply lime to remedy this.

**Magnesium deficiency** is often the cause of poor coloured, yellowing foliage. Epsom Salts applied at the rate of $\frac{1}{2}$ oz. to a gallon of water will put this right.

**Boron deficiency** leads to bushy, irregular growth with the terminal shoots curling. Apply Borax.

**Iron deficiency** leads to lack of stamina and often, poor looking plants. It is unlikely to occur where the soil has been dressed with manure, compost and other organic matter.

Deficiency diseases will not occur if the soil is in good condition and well fed since they will then contain both the main feeding agents and trace elements. Sometimes roots are unable to absorb the nutrients. This could be due to a packed down, airless soil or to an excess or absence of lime, for/ some plants need calcareous soil and others an alkaline rooting medium.

# CHAPTER ELEVEN

# *Organic Fertilizers and Manures*

Now that bulky animal manures and night soils are rarely obtainable we have to depend on other feeding agencies. Fortunately there are many of a natural origin including the following.

## Those Supplying Nitrogen

*Dried Blood*. Fairly quick lasting. Scatter on the surface and work in or use as a liquid.

*Hoof and Horn meal*. Slow in action and releases its value over a long period.

*Shoddy*. Slow and varying greatly in its value. Can be used as a base dressing before planting.

*Soot*. Fairly rapid, should be well weathered. Scatter and work well into the soil or use as a liquid.

*Leather Dust*. Used when finely ground, this can be most useful although somewhat difficult to obtain.

## Supply Phosphorus

*Steamed Bone Flour*. Useful as a top dressing and for working in.

*Bone Meal*. Slow in action but a valued all round organic feed releasing its nourishment gradually over a long period.

## Supplying Potash

*Wood Ash*. Of fairly rapid availability. Must be kept well covered and dry until required. Its value varies according to the wood.

## Supplying Several Plant Foods

*Castor Oil Meal*. This supplies nitrogen, phosphorus and potash. It should be scattered on the surface and worked into the soil.

*Guanos* are the residue of the excreta of fish eating birds. They are quick in action and richer than poultry manure.

*Meat and Bone Meal*, often known as tankage or meat meal. This provides nitrogen and some phosphorus. Use it as a base dressing, working it in well.

*Fish Manure*. A very safe fertiliser useful for a wide range of plants. Apply three to four oz. to the square yard.

*Poultry Manure*. Releases its feeding value over a long period but should be composted, stacked or stored and kept dry until required.

*Farmyard manure*. Difficult to obtain but undoubtedly invaluable in that it adds bulk as well as supplying nitrogen, phosphorus, potash and other feeding matter. Should be worked in and not left on the surface.

*Rape Meal*. Slow in action. Useful for top dressing.

*Spent Hops*. Useful for supplying bulk as well as for its food value. It may be dug in at the rate of a large bucketful to the square yard.

*Sewage Sludge*. This varies greatly in its feeding and organic content, although several local authorities are now able to give an analysis. It is useful for improving the physical condition of the soil rather than for its supply of nourishment.

*Seaweed*. Slow acting but entirely reliable containing all the major and minor trace elements. Useful for adding to the compost heap especially the drift weed and bladderwrack varieties. In its powder and liquid forms, it is an invaluable feed for all vegetables.

# Trace Elements

Trace elements are needed by plants, animals and man in a number of ways – quite how many, nobody knows. But there is one way in which trace elements are known to be essential, and that is in forming part of the enzymes which initiate and control many of the processes vital to the plant. One of these is the use of carbon produced by photosynthesis to help make fats and sugars.

Trace elements have been long accepted in gardening circles as highly beneficial. In Maxicrop, a seaweed fertiliser, they are present in the best proportions and forms for application. Maxicrop is made chiefly from Ascophyllum nodosum (bladder wrack). Seaweed contains all the fifty-five trace elements present in this substance, and it contains them in a 'chelated' form which enables the plant to absorb them directly. This means the plant is getting all the trace elements in a far more effective manner than if they were precipitated in solution, and in the natural proportions controlled naturally by the sea.

This is important because it can be dangerous to give an overdoze of a particular trace element. The elements in Maxicrop, having already been absorbed by the seaweed, have been proved to be in ideal proportions. An important role of trace elements is to replace deficiencies in plants. We can look at deficiencies from the point of symptoms, and the role of the element in the normal plant.

## The main trace elements are the following:

*Magnesium* is a mobile nutrient like nitrogen and phosphorus. When deficiency occurs, it appears first in the old leaves since these yield up their stock to the younger leaves. Since magnesium is an essential component of chlorophyll, deficiency results not unnaturally in chlorosis. However, brilliant tints may appear in the foliage in addition to the chlorosis.

*Calcium* is necessary to bind the cells of the plant together. This may be the reason why calcium deficiency causes an inhibition of bud development and the death of the root tips, since cell division is most active in these regions. Thus with calcium deficiency the young leaves may become distorted, the tips hooked back and the margins curled and ragged. Scorching may also be apparent. The root systems of such plants are poorly developed and often appear gelatinous. Symptoms vary according to the actual level of deficiency and also with the plant species involved. Calcium deficiency most commonly occurs in acid soils.

*Sulphur* is necessary for protein formation, in vitamins and in enzymes. Its absence results in reduced growth of the shoots, and the leaves may be tinted or yellowed. Perhaps due to the protein deficiency the stems become stuff, woody and thin.

*Iron* plays a crucial role in chlorophyll formation. Most growers, are familiar with iron deficiency and many of them have been helped to combat it by Maxicrop complexed with iron. It appears as severe chlorosis, young growth being the worst affected. Deficiencies are common in soils of a high lime content where it is referred to as 'lime induced chlorosis'.

*Boron deficiency* is not common but its lack may result in several disorders involving disintegration of plant tissue. Death of the stem and of the root tips occurs in many cases. The latter may be related to its suspected role in carbohydrate transport.

*Manganese deficiency* is also not common. When it does occur, it appears as an interveinal chlorosis followed by necrotic lesions, which may be connected with its role in the chloroplast membrane system.

*Molybdenum* is required in smaller amounts than the other elements although its deficiency is widespread. It has been known to lead to 'whiptail' in cauliflowers and broccoli.

*Zinc* is important in a number of enzymes and its absence results in a decrease in leaf size and in the length between the internodes. Stem growth is retarded partly due to the absence of zinc causing a reduction in hormone acid, which is necessary for the normal enlargement of the cells of the stem.

*Copper deficiency* is rare. Young leaves become dark green, twisted and encrotic spots appear.

Apart from these major trace elements there are others needed in much smaller amounts. These are usually present in well cultivated and fed soil. They include iodine, bromine, soda, cobalt, nickel and alumina. Seaweed is a source of all of these properties as well as minute quantities of beryllium, selenium, tungsten, and various other minerals. Seaweed varies in its constituent form from season to season, so that an analysis would be bound to vary in different years. But seaweed fertilisers can be recommended in view of their make-up.

Manufacturers say that a typical sample of dry seaweed manure contains 13% water, 2% nitrogen, 63% humus forming materials and alignates, with 22% mineral matter.

## Foliar Feeding

Although the long accepted way of feeding plants has been through the roots, foliar feeding is a method by which plant nutrients are supplied to the plant via the leaves, rather than the roots.

It was observed as early as the 1880's that plant metabolites could be leached from the leaves by rain. And so it was proposed that if plant substances could move out of the leaf, could they not equally simply move in the reverse direction, that is, into the leaf.

Studies with fluorescent materials, which act as dies, and radioactive tracers enabled research workers to follow the passage of plant nutrients through the leaves and into the plant system, and also to determine the rate at which they travel. In this way the absorption of nutrients by the leaves has been established. These techniques, not only showed that plants can absorb nutrients through their leaves but also gave an indication of the rate at which nutrients are absorbed therein.

Work using beans, showed that significant absorption takes place within as little as ten minutes after application and that after thirty minutes, an appreciable amount of the substances sprayed on the leaf have been absorbed.

There appears to be no conclusive evidence as to the manner in which nutrients enter the leaf. Entry is thought to be possible by two routes. One is through the imperforated cuticle and an alternative, through breaks in the cuticle, such as the stomata and the hydathodes.

The upper and lower surfaces of leaves are covered initially by single layers of flattened epidermal cells. The main purpose of these cells is protection. The epidermis – this layer of epidermal cells – is so thin that transpiration can take place through it, but before the leaf is very old a layer of a substance called cutin forms over the surface of the leaf and prevents further transpiration. This continuous covering of cutin, which is a resistant fatty material, renders the outer walls of the leaves more or less water and gas tight. Very often the cuticle is coated with wax, which increases this water and gas resistance. This wax is present to a high degree in evergreens and given these leaves their characteristic shiny appearance.

It is thought that plant nutrients sprayed on to the leaf might be absorbed to some extent through this treble protective layer – first the wax, then the cuticle, and then the epidermal cells. This could occur by the process of diffusion if this protective layer exhibits a degree of permeability. Permeable membranes are those which allow certain materials to pass through them. This occurs when such materials are present in greater concentrations on one side than on the other; Then they pass through to the side in which they are present in less concentration. It is possible that this is one way in which plant nutrients could be absorbed by the leaf.

However, it is more likely that nutrients are absorbed through natural breaks in the leaf. The most common of these are the stomata, which are slit-like openings between two guard cells. The guard cells enable the stomata to be opened and closed. The purpose of the stomata is gaseous interchange; carbon dioxide finds its way into the leaf via the stomata and oxygen finds its way out of the leaf. It has been suggested that the plant nutrients could find their way into the leaf through the stomata, but there is one obstacle in the path of this argument. This is that the guard cells which surround the stomata are so shaped as to make the entry of water impossible unless it is forced in under pressure. The guard cells give the stomata such a shape that drops of water are unable to pass through. If it were the case that plant nutrients were being absorbed by the stomata, then anything which reduced the size of the water droplets should increase the absorption of the foliar nutrients.

There are other natural openings in the leaf, for example the hydathodes which are water secreting glands, which are present on the edges and tips of the leaves. However, these are not present nearly as frequently as stomata and not nearly sufficiently quantitively to be the route for the considerable absorption of foliar sprays that takes place.

Despite the paucity of fundamental understanding a considerable amount is known about the absorption of various nutrients. For instance, urea nitrogen is absorbed, transported, and metabolized as quickly as any plant nutrient. Uptake of urea is most rapid at night or in the early morning – this could be due to the higher relative humidity of the air at this time. The elements sulphur, chlorine, and iodine are known to be very rapidly absorbed. Whereas the rate of absorption of magnesium varies during the day, it is better absorbed at night. Magnesium calcium, strontium and beryllium have a rapid initial absorption, but this is followed by the failure of the plant to absorb any more. Iron, manganese, zinc, copper, molybdenum, and cobalt act in the same way. This is thought to be because these elements have a limited mobility within the plant and become accumulated in the leaf.

Absorption rates are greater for young leaves than older leaves and usually absorption is greater on the underside of the leaf than on the exposed surface.

Foliar feeds have a wide and diverse range of activities. They increase yield, improve quality, increase resistance to pests and diseases and extend storage life.

# Appendix I:

# Glossary of Botanical Terms

| | |
|---|---|
| Adventitous roots. | Roots arising from beds forming in other than normal places. |
| Anthers. | The pollen bearing part of the stamen. |
| Aromatic. | Fragrant in parts, other than the flowers. |
| Basal. | Situate or growing at the base = basal shoot. |
| Bigeneric | One obtained by crossing two genera. |
| Blade. | An expanded leaf or petal. |
| Bract. | The small scale-like leaves below the flower. |
| Calcifuge. | Intolerant of lime. |
| Calyx. | The outer part immediately enveloping the flower. |
| Cultivar. | Hybrids or varieties arising under cultivation. |
| Diploid. | Having two sets of chromosomes. |
| Ecology. | The study of plants in relation to their environment. |
| Endemic. | Native to a locality or country. |
| Epidermis. | The outer layer of cells. |
| Eye. | A bud as seen in a potato tuber. |
| Fasciated. | Having an abnormal stem or flower where the plants have flattened or joined together. |
| Fertile. | Land in good heart, *or* seed able to germinate. |
| Glaucous. | Dull greyish-green or greyish-blue. |
| Habitat. | Natural home of a plant. |
| Hermaphrodite. | Having flowers with both male and female parts. |
| Hilum. | The point on a seed where it's joined to the seed case. |
| Inflorescence. | The flower or flower cluster. |
| Internode. | The stem between two consecutive nodes. |
| Laciniate. | Of leaves deeply cut into narrow lobes. |
| Legume. | A member of Leguminosae, for example peas. |
| Mycorrhiza. | The association of a plant's roots with a fungus. |

| | | | |
|---|---|---|---|
| Node. | A joint where a bud or leaf is produced. | Stamen. | The pollen bearing male organ. |
| Ovule. | The part of a pistil which becomes seed after pollinating. | Stigma. | The part of the pistil which receives pollen from the stem. |
| Palmate. | Leaves lobed in the shape of a hand. | Stolon. | A stem issuing horizontally below ground. |
| Raceme. | A cluster of flowers having stems issuing from a main stem. | Tunicate. | Composed of layers or scales, as in onions. |
| Species. | A plant which comes true from seed. | Variant. | Differing in minor ways from the species. |

# Appendix II

# *Climatic Maps*

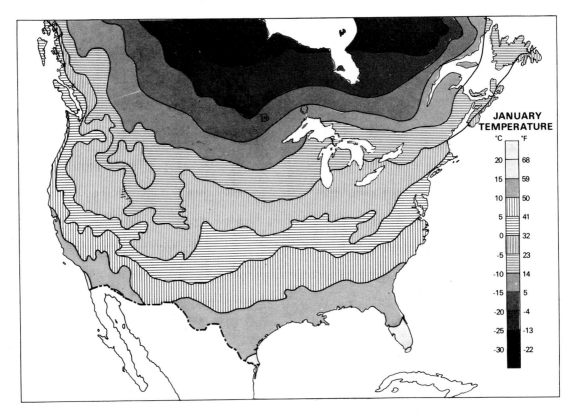

JANUARY TEMPERATURE

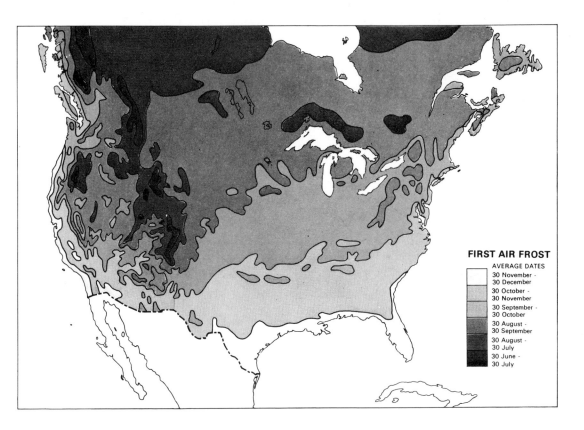

**FIRST AIR FROST**

AVERAGE DATES

- 30 November - 30 December
- 30 October - 30 November
- 30 September - 30 October
- 30 August - 30 September
- 30 August - 30 July
- 30 June - 30 July

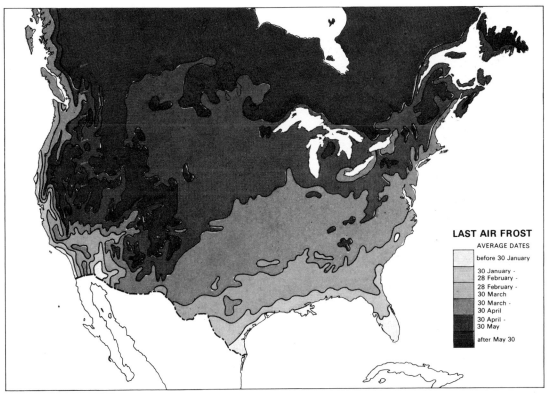

**LAST AIR FROST**

AVERAGE DATES

- before 30 January
- 30 January - 28 February
- 28 February - 30 March
- 30 March - 30 April
- 30 April - 30 May
- after May 30

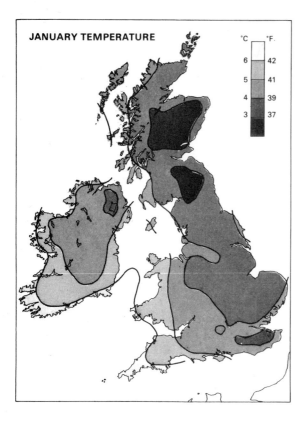

**JANUARY TEMPERATURE**

| °C | °F |
|----|----|
| 6 | 42 |
| 5 | 41 |
| 4 | 39 |
| 3 | 37 |

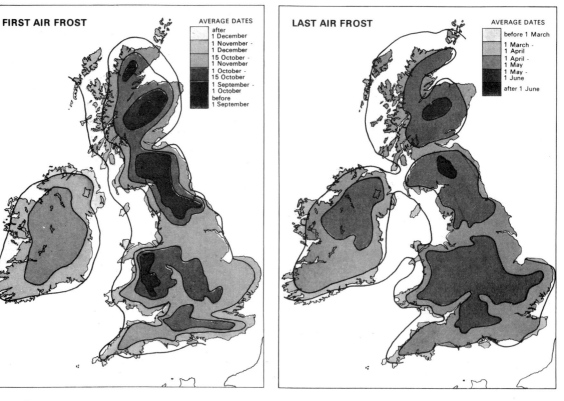

**FIRST AIR FROST**

AVERAGE DATES
after
1 December
1 November -
1 December
15 October -
1 November
1 October -
15 October
1 September -
1 October
before
1 September

**LAST AIR FROST**

AVERAGE DATES
before 1 March
1 March -
1 April
1 April -
1 May
1 May -
1 June
after 1 June

# Appendix III
# *The Seasons Chart*

| | Hardiness | Depth | Time to sow |
|---|---|---|---|
| Asparagus | Hardy | 1½ in' | 2 weeks after last frost |
| Butter Beans | Tender | 1½ in. | 4 weeks after last frost |
| Broad Beans, English or Fava | Hardy | 2½ in. | 4 weeks before last frost |
| Runner Beans | Semi-hardy | 2–3 in. | 3 weeks after last frost |
| Snap Beans, French, Kidney, or String | Tender | 1½ in. | 8 weeks after last frost |
| Beets | Semi-hardy | 1 in. | Just after last frost |
| Broccoli | Semi-hardy | ½ in. | 3 weeks after last frost |
| Brussels Sprouts | Hardy | ½ in. | 2 weeks after last frost |
| Cabbage | Hardy | ½ in. | Fall/Winter: 4, 8, 12 weeks after last frost |
| Carrots | Hardy | ¼ in. | July for fall crop and last frost date |
| Cauliflower | Semi-hardy | ½ in. | Indoors: 6 weeks before last frost date; Outdoors: 2 weeks after last frost |
| Celery | Semi-hardy | ¼ in. | 4 weeks before last frost |
| Cucumber | Tender | 1 in. | 4–6 weeks before transplant date |
| Eggplant, Aubergine | Tender | ½ in. | Outdoors: 4 weeks after last frost |
| Kohlrabi | Semi-hardy | ½ in. | Last frost date |
| Leeks | Hardy | 1 in. | Outdoors: 4 weeks before last frost; Indoors: 6 weeks before last frost |
| Lettuce | Semi-hardy | ½ in. | First sowing 2 weeks after last frost |
| Marrows and Squashes | Semi-hardy | 1 in. | Outdoors: 4–6 weeks after last frost; Indoors: 1–2 weeks after last frost |
| Melons (Cantaloupes) | Semi-hardy | 1 in. | Outdoors (in USA): 4–6 weeks after last frost. Indoors: 1 week after last frost |
| Onion | Hardy | ½ in. | Outdoors: last frost date; Indoors: 8 weeks before last frost |
| Peas (English, Edible podded, Snow or Sugar) | Hardy | 2 in. | Last frost date |
| Peppers, Sweet and Hot | Tender | ¼ in. | Indoors: 4 weeks before last frost date; Outdoors: 4 weeks after last frost |
| Potato, White | Semi-hardy | 4 in. | 2 weeks before last frost |
| Pumpkins | Tender | 1½ in. | Outdoors: 4–6 weeks after last frost; Indoors: 3–4 weeks after last frost |
| Radish | Hardy | ½ in. | First sowing last frost date |
| Shallots | Hardy | 1 in. | Last frost date |
| Spinach | Hardy | ½ in. | 4 weeks before last frost |
| Swiss Chard (Seakale Beet) | Semi-hardy | 1 in. | Last frost date |
| Tomato | Tender | ½ in. | Outdoors: 4 weeks after last frost; Indoors: 1–3 weeks before last frost |

# Appendix IV:

# *Weights and Measures*

| | Approx. No. of seeds per oz. | Average Germination Period. | Average Germination Percentage | Viability under good storage |
|---|---|---|---|---|
| Asparagus | 1600 | 23–35 days | 95% | 3–7 years |
| Aubergine (Egg Plant) | 6700 | 7 days | 70% | 4–5 years |
| Beans (Broad) | 17 | 7–10 days | 96% | 5 years |
| Beans (French) | 40 | 5–10 days | 94% | 3–4 years |
| Beans (Haricot) | 40 | 5–10 days | 94% | 3–4 years |
| Beans (Runner) | 30–40 | 7–10 days | 94% | 3–4 years |
| Beetroot | 1400 | 10–14 days | 90% | 4 years |
| Broccoli | 10,500 | 5–10 days | 90% | 4–5 years |
| Brussels Sprouts | 11,200 | 12 days | 90% | 4–5 years |
| Cabbage (Green) | 7000 | 12 days | 85–90% | 4 years |
| Cabbage (Red) | 8400 | 12 days | 85–90% | 4 years |
| Cabbage (Savoy) | 7000 | 12 days | 85–90% | 4 years |
| Cardoon | 650 | 12–16 days | 93% | 5–8 years |
| Carrots (cleaned seed) | 25,000 | 7–20 days | 70% | 3–4 years |
| Cauliflower | 14,000 | 4–7 days | 87% | 4 years |
| Celeriac | 84,000 | 12 days | 75% | 3–6 years |
| Celery | 84,000 | 12 days | 75% | 3–6 years |
| Chicory (Witloof) | 19,500 | 7–14 days | 75–85% | 4–5 years |
| Cress (Garden) | 15,000 | 1–3 days | 98% | 3–4 years |
| Cucumber | 1100 | 3 days | 95% | 8 years |
| Endive | 19,500 | 3–6 days | 85% | 4 years |
| Gherkin | 1100 | 3 days | 95% | 8 years |
| Kale | 12,000 | 7–10 days | 85–90% | 4 years |
| Leek | 9800 | 12 days | 84% | 2–4 years |
| Lettuce | 35,000 | 4–10 days | 85% | 4 years |

| | Approx. No. of seed per oz. | Average Germination Period | Average Germination Percentage | Viability under good storage |
|---|---|---|---|---|
| Marrow | 65–140 | 6–8 days | 80% | 5–8 years |
| Melons | 850 | 4–5 days | 95% | 8 years |
| Onion (salad) | 8–10,000 | 12–20 days | 85% | 2–3 years |
| Onion (bulb) | 8–10,000 | 12–20 days | 85% | 2–3 years |
| Parsley | 15,000 | 10–21 days | 76% | 2–3 years |
| Parsnip | 7000 | 21 days | 60–70% | 1–2 years |
| Pea | 225 | 9 days | 90–95% | 3–6 years |
| Pea (sugar) | 225 | 9 days | 90–95% | 3–6 years |
| Purslane | 64,000 | 4 days | 90% | 3–4 years |
| Radish | 2800 | 5–7 days | 88% | 4–5 years |
| Radish (winter) | 2800 | 9 days | 88% | 4–5 years |
| Salsify | 2800 | 14–20 days | 90% | 2–4 years |
| Scorzonera | 2000 | 8–14 days | 88% | 1–2 years |
| Spinach | 2500 | 8–14 days | 92% | 4–5 years |
| Spinach Beet (Swiss Chard) | 1950 | 14 days | 90% | 4 years |
| Swede | 10,000 | 2–10 days | 90% | 3–5 years |
| Sweet Corn | 85 | 7 days | 85% | 2 years |
| Tomato | 7–9000 | 7–10 days | 91% | 4–6 years |
| Turnip | 12,500 | 2–10 days | 90% | 3–5 years |

## Vitamin and Protein content of some Vegetables

| | Vitamins | Protein | | Vitamins | Protein |
|---|---|---|---|---|---|
| Green Peas | A, B, C | High | Cauliflowers | A, B, C | Low |
| Dwarf French Beans | A, B, C | Low | Cucumber | B & C | Low |
| Broad Beans | A, B, C | Medium | Lettuce | A, B, C & E | Low |
| Brussels Sprouts | A, B, C | Medium | Melons | A, B, C | Low |
| Carrots | A, B, C & E | Low | Onions | B & C | Low |
| Courgette | B & C | Low | Sweet Corn | A & B | High |
| Cabbage | A, B, C | Low | Radishes | A, B, C | Low |

# Useful Conversion Tables

| Litre | Gallons | Gallons | Litres | cm | Inches | Metres | Yards | Inches | cm |
|---|---|---|---|---|---|---|---|---|---|
| 1 = | 0.220 | 1 = | 4.546 | 1 = | 0.394 | 1 = | 1.094 | 1 = | 2.540 |
| 2 = | 0.440 | 2 = | 9.092 | 2 = | 0.787 | 2 = | 2.187 | 2 = | 5.080 |
| 3 = | 0.660 | 3 = | 13.638 | 3 = | 1.181 | 3 = | 3.281 | 3 = | 7.620 |
| 4 = | 0.880 | 4 = | 18.184 | 4 = | 1.575 | 4 = | 4.374 | 4 = | 10.160 |
| 5 = | 1.100 | 5 = | 22.730 | 5 = | 1.969 | 5 = | 5.468 | 5 = | 12.700 |
| 6 = | 1.320 | 6 = | 27.276 | 6 = | 2.362 | 6 = | 6.562 | 6 = | 15.240 |
| 7 = | 1.540 | 7 = | 31.822 | 7 = | 2.756 | 7 = | 7.655 | 7 = | 17.780 |
| 8 = | 1.760 | 8 = | 36.368 | 8 = | 3.150 | 8 = | 8.749 | 8 = | 20.320 |
| 9 = | 1.980 | 9 = | 40.914 | 9 = | 3.543 | 9 = | 9.843 | 9 = | 22.860 |
| 10 = | 2.200 | 10 = | 45.460 | 10 = | 3.937 | 10 = | 10.936 | 10 = | 25.400 |
| 20 = | 4.400 | 20 = | 90.919 | 20 = | 7.874 | 20 = | 21.872 | 20 = | 50.800 |
| 30 = | 6.599 | 30 = | 136.379 | 30 = | 11.811 | 30 = | 32.808 | 30 = | 76.200 |
| 40 = | 8.799 | 40 = | 181.839 | 40 = | 15.748 | 40 = | 43.745 | 40 = | 101.600 |
| 50 = | 10.999 | 50 = | 227.298 | 50 = | 19.685 | 50 = | 54.681 | 50 = | 127.000 |
| 60 = | 13.199 | 60 = | 272.758 | 60 = | 23.622 | 60 = | 65.617 | 60 = | 152.400 |
| 70 = | 15.398 | 70 = | 318.217 | 70 = | 27.599 | 70 = | 76.553 | 70 = | 177.800 |
| 80 = | 17.598 | 80 = | 363.677 | 80 = | 31.496 | 80 = | 87.489 | 80 = | 203.200 |
| 90 = | 19.798 | 90 = | 409.137 | 90 = | 35.433 | 90 = | 98.425 | 90 = | 228.600 |
| 100 = | 21.998 | 100 = | 454.596 | 100 = | 39.370 | 100 = | 109.361 | 100 = | 254.000 |

1 gal = 8 pints

| Kilogrammes | Pounds | Kilogrammes | Pounds |
|---|---|---|---|
| 1 = | 2.205 | 20 = | 44.092 |
| 2 = | 4.409 | 30 = | 66.139 |
| 3 = | 6.614 | 40 = | 88.185 |
| 4 = | 8.819 | 50 = | 110.231 |
| 5 = | 11.023 | 60 = | 132.277 |
| 6 = | 13.228 | 70 = | 154.324 |
| 7 = | 15.432 | 80 = | 176.370 |
| 8 = | 17.637 | 90 = | 198.416 |
| 9 = | 19.842 | 100 = | 220.462 |
| 10 = | 22.046 | | |

# Appendix V
## Useful Addresses

Adco Ltd.,
Harpenden,
Hertfordshire.

Adco Compost Maker.

Albright & Wilson Ltd.,
Farm Protection Ltd.,
Glaston Park,
Uppingham,
Leicestershire.

Siapton Organic
Foliar Feed.

Alexander Products Ltd.,
Ashcott,
Burnham on Sea,
Somerset.

Peat products and
Tom Bags.

Bugge's Insecticides Ltd.,
Sittingbourne,
Kent.

Liquid Derris.
Pidero pesticide.
Miscible Concentrated
mixture of Derris and
Pyrethrum.

Chase Organics,
Gibraltar House,
Shepperton,
Middlesex.
TW17 8AG.

Composts, peats,
Seaweed products, etc.

Chase Compost Seeds Ltd.,
Benhall,
Saxmundham,
Suffolk.

Compost grown
flower and vegetable
seeds.

Henry Doubleday
Research Association,
20, Convent Lane,
Bocking,
Braintree,
Essex.

Comfrey plants for
composting.

D. L. Coutts
(Horticultural) Ltd.,
Roundstone Lane,
Angmering on Sea,
Sussex.

Clavering Compost
Laced with seaweed.

Farmura Ltd.,
Stonehill,
Egerton,
Nr. Ashford,
Kent.

Farmura Organic
manure and foliar feed.

Fertosan Ltd.,
Wolverhampton.

Fertosan Compost
Accelerator.

Garotta Products Ltd.,
Station Mills,
Bute Street,
Luton,
LU1 2HE.

Garotta compost
maker.

Hempsall Ltd.,
Walesby,
Newark,
Notts.

Organic fertilisers.

Humber Manures Ltd.,
Stoneferry,
Hull.
HU8 8DQ.

Humber organic
manures.

Hunters of Chester Ltd.,
Chester.

Organically grown
seeds.

Maxicrop Ltd.,
Neptune House,
Holdenby,
Northampton.

Maxicrop, Seaweed
fertiliser.

Murphy's Cowpact,
Tyrells Manor Farm,
Stoke Hammond,
Milton Keynes,
Buckinghamshire.
MK17 9BX.

Cowpact. Natural
organic fertiliser,
powder and liquid,
from Cow Manure.

Organic Concentrates Ltd.,
Chalfont St. Giles,
Bucks.

6X Concentrated
manure.

Organic Farmers &
Growers Ltd.,
Longridge,
Creeting Road,
Stowmarket,
Suffolk.

Siapton Spray.
Organic foliar feed.

Pelco Organic Fertilisers
Ltd.,
West Kington,
Chippenham,
Wilts.

Boost concentrated
organic manure.

P.R.M. Horticultural
Services Ltd.,
3, Woodrise, Eastcote,
Pinner,
Middlesex.

Fertile,
Organic concentrated
fertiliser.

L. & S. Powling,
Stallage Common,
Ippleden,
Newton Abbot,
Devon.

Organic Fertiliser,
Leaf Mould.

Wilfred Smith Ltd.,
Gemini House,
High Street,
Edgware,
Middlesex.
HA8 7ET.

Marinure Liquid
seaweed.

*Surrey Loams Ltd.,*
Farnham,
Surrey.

Bark based composts.
For top dressing and
growing bags.

*Seaweed Agricultural Ltd.,*
Holdenby,
Northamptonshire.

Neptunes Bounty
Seaweed.

## Great Britain.

*The Soil Association,*
Walnut Tree Farm,
Haughley,
Stowmarket,
Suffolk.
*Henry Doubleday Research Association,*
20, Convent Lane,
Bocking,
Braintree,
Essex.

## United States.

*Soil and Health Foundation,*
46, South West Street,
Allentown,
Pennsylvania.

## Australia.

*Henry Doubleday Australian Group,*
Greggs Road,
Kurrajong,
New South Wales.

## Canada.

*Canadian Soil Association of Organic Husbandry,*
116, Joicey Boulevard,
Toronto 12,
Ontario,
Canada.

## New Zealand.

*Organic Compost Society Inc.,*
27, Collins Street,
Addington,
Christchurch,
New Zealand.

## South Africa.

*Soil Association of South Africa,*
Box 47100, P.O. Parklands,
Johannesburg.

# Index